How to
Make Money
from Freelance
Writing

ANDREW CROFTS

How to Make Money from Freelance Writing

PIATKUS

Copyright © 1992 Andrew Crofts

First published 1992 by Judy Piatkus (Publishers) Ltd,
5 Windmill Street, London W1P 1HF

First paperback edition 1993
This edition revised and updated 1997

The moral right of the author has been asserted

*A catalogue record for this book is available
from the British Library*

ISBN 0 7499 1233 2

Typeset in Compugraphic Times by
Action Typesetting Ltd, Gloucester
Printed and bound in Great Britain by
Biddles Ltd, Guildford and King's Lynn

Contents

Introduction

I may be biased, but I happen to think that being a freelance writer is the most wonderful way of earning a living. There is nothing, except perhaps inherited wealth, which provides greater personal freedom and flexibility.

Being a professional writer allows you to follow your own interests and develop yourself in any direction you choose. It gives you the freedom to live where you want and how you want, and to travel wherever and whenever the urge takes you. As a freelancer you never know when luck is going to drop some wonderful opportunity into your lap.

Every morning when you wake up you know that something exciting may happen today. Maybe a publisher will ring up with a really big commission, a novel might be accepted, a huge star might agree to an interview, a magazine might buy an article or send you to Tahiti with all expenses paid, the film rights to a book could sell for thousands, or a major chat show host will want to interview you.

Most days, of course, nothing happens, except more work. But every so often something comes along which reminds you of just how much *is* possible.

I have been a freelance writer for nearly twenty-five years now, ever since I left school, and I have tried my hand at virtually every type of writing. Sometimes my efforts have paid off, at other times they have led me up blind alleys. And I have received my share of rejections along the way.

I have worked as a journalist, a non-fiction author, a novelist and short-story writer, a travel writer, a business writer, a ghostwriter and a scriptwriter. I have sold articles to most of the national papers, all the way from the quality press to the tabloids, as well as to a wide range of consumer, business and trade journals.

I have been able to travel to every part of the world that I have wanted to visit, and have been shown enormous hospitality by the people I have met. I have been able to discover worlds which I would never have known about, and to meet people that I would otherwise only have read about or seen on the television screen.

Freelance writing is a way of life which I can wholeheartedly recommend to anyone who enjoys variety and who likes to have reasonable control of their own destiny.

I hope this book will convey some of the pleasures of freelancing at the same time as explaining how to make a living at it. I hope it will also help those who are trying to get their work published, to bear the early rejections and disappointments philosophically, knowing that, with perseverance, they can achieve whatever they want.

Andrew Crofts

1

Why be a Freelance Writer?

*No man but a blockhead
ever wrote, except for money.*
SAMUEL JOHNSON, 1776

A freelance writer is anyone who sells their work to others on an *ad hoc* basis. That means everyone from Hollywood screenwriters to the gardening correspondents on the local papers, from people who make millions a year from blockbuster novels, to people who make a few hundred pounds selling the occasional article or short story.

Some of us choose to make a full-time living from the craft, while others just use it to supplement their incomes. The latter could be anyone from full-time journalists who write books and sell articles to other publishers in their spare time, to housewives looking for some extra income. Many freelance writers are experts in a particular subject – perhaps law or gardening, embroidery or the Soviet Union – and one of the ways they use their skills and experiences is to write about them. They might be university professors or market gardeners, chefs or interior decorators, golfers or politicians, business people or doctors.

This book is aimed at helping those who have found that they enjoy writing, and who believe that they are good at it, to market their wares. I would not presume to tell anyone *how* to write. I just hope to give those who *can* a better idea of how to make a living from their skills.

LEARN HOW TO MAKE MONEY FIRST

When I first told my parents that I wanted to be a writer they were naturally fearful for me, knowing enough to worry about the unpredictability and insecurity involved but not enough to offer me much practical advice. They told an old family friend – a man who had made several fortunes – about my ambitions.

'That's all fine,' he said, 'but tell him to learn how to make money first.'

That is what this book is about, because unless you learn how to sell your writing to other people you will soon become disillusioned and give up trying. If you were hoping to be a full-time writer you will be forced to give up before your talent has emerged. Even if you just want to treat it as a hobby, you will soon become disillusioned if no one appreciates your work enough to pay you for it.

PURSUING YOUR DREAMS

You don't necessarily have to give up your dreams of producing some great creative work in order to earn a crust. Provided you are businesslike in your approach, there is no reason why your writing cannot be used to pay for any lifestyle you want, and give you the time to write 'for yourself' as well as for your clients. As a professional writer you will be constantly honing your skills, which will in turn help to improve the work you ultimately want to do.

Everyone has to start by serving an apprenticeship, whatever profession they are in. Few people will start their careers by writing *Pride and Prejudice* or *Gone with the Wind*. Most great works are produced when the creators have been toiling at their craft for many years.

Becoming a successful freelance writer has a lot to do with determination and persistence. And in order to make the necessary effort you need to be sure that the freelance life is what you really want. It may help to have a brief look at the pros and cons and the personal qualities you will need.

THE ADVANTAGES OF BEING A FREELANCE WRITER

1 The Chance to Follow Your Interests

If you are passionately concerned about Third World poverty, you can get out there to chronicle it. If you are more interested in the lifestyles of the rich and famous, you can follow your prey to their glamorous watering holes around the world, and satisfy your curiosity about every detail of their lives. If you are keen on model railways you can spend your days searching out wonderful collections and writing about them.

Writers can get themselves invited to palaces or war zones, brothels or nunneries. And they can get to meet the greatest heroes and villains of our time. Whenever you read an article or a non-fiction book about someone or something which thrills or absorbs you, you know that in most cases the writer actually had that first-hand experience which they are now passing on to you; they flew that little bit higher.

2 The Freedom to Stay at Home

At the same time as giving you the freedom to go anywhere in the world and see anything you choose, freelancing also allows you to stay at home. Fully employed mortals have to fight their way through rush hour traffic at the same time every day, and on to crowded railway platforms, simply in order to be 'somewhere else', even though that somewhere may be an unappealing office full of people they would rather not spend the day with. But the freelancer can stay at home and organise his working hours to fit in with private or family life.

Of course there will be days when you have to go somewhere in order to get a prized job or a vital interview, but there is no routine travel involved.

The futurologists, writing about how our working practices will change in the next few decades, are predicting that most people will spend more time working from home, with the help of telecommunications and computing technology. Freelance writers are already doing it.

Some might find that there are too many distractions at home. If so, they can set up working arrangements to suit their own inclinations. One option is to rent an office or some shared office space so that you can work elsewhere when the pressures of family life become too great. Another solution is to write about subjects which involve you in a lot of travel. The point is – the choice is yours.

3   The Chance to Stay on the Learning Curve

I understand 'the learning curve' to mean the rate at which we progress from our natural state of ignorance about everything to a knowledgeable understanding of one or more subjects.

For most people, the learning curve is steepest when they are young. Many people reach the top of their work learning curve in their twenties or thirties. They are then qualified to practise their trade or profession. As they stop learning new things they cease to be stimulated by their work, and life loses much of its zest and excitement.

Some people, however, are lucky enough to be in professions which keep them on a continuous learning curve. Others take up hobbies and special interests which compensate for anything that might be lacking in their working lives. Freelance writers can continue learning indefinitely about everything that interests them. Furthermore, they can utilise their interests and hobbies in their work. As soon as they have mastered one subject to a level which gives them satisfaction, they can move on to another, developing and improving themselves constantly as they go.

4   The Joy of Working for Yourself

The next great advantage is the one shared by many other self-employed professions – the joy of being able to work for yourself. Provided you earn enough money to meet your immediate needs, you can do whatever you want. There is no boss to tell you when you should start work and when you should finish.

Of course there will be customers in the form of publishers, editors and others, who will put certain conditions on how you present the work which they commission from you, but these are small compromises compared to the ones endured by someone who has their entire salary paid by one person.

There will also be deadlines to meet, but provided you are disciplined in your work there is no reason why you shouldn't choose when and where you want to do the work. If you want to take the day off because the sun is shining, and do the work in the evening, or early the next morning, the choice is yours.

5   *The Chance to Communicate*

Many people who write for a living don't so much choose to do it as know that there is nothing else they really want to do. Even if they are distracted by other things for a while, they will end up going back to writing sooner or later.

It is a wonderful feeling to find out something which really interests you, and then to be able to pass the news on to other people. Writers are usually people who like the sound of their own voices, who like to pass on, explain or show off what they have learned. Some writers have a burning need to voice their own opinions, but most simply want to discover things about the world and then chat about them to others. Instead of doing it in the local pub or over the back fence, they do it in print or over the airwaves.

6   *The Security of Working for Several Employers*

Anyone who has a full-time job only has to upset one employer and they lose their entire livelihood; likewise, the person whose company gets into financial difficulties and who then finds themselves out of work. A freelance writer, however, might be working for three different book publishers, several magazine editors and a number of public relations, film and television companies. That makes him or her much less vulnerable than the person with one 'steady' job.

7 *The Status*

Perhaps we should also admit that there is just a hint of pride involved in being a professional writer, as long as you are successful.

The word 'writer' often makes people think of best-selling novelists and screenwriters, or famous columnists from the national papers, and their interest wanes very quickly when they discover that they have never heard your name or read anything you have written.

Even so, they will probably still be more interested in talking to a writer than yet another accountant or secretary.

THE QUALITIES A FREELANCE WRITER NEEDS

The more of these attributes you have, the greater your chance of succeeding as a freelance writer.

1 *Self-Discipline*

There is no one else to tell you to get on with your work. If you can't make yourself sit down and do it when it needs to be done you will not be able to earn a living.

2 *The Ability to Cope with Financial Insecurity*

Some people are very worried by the idea of not having a regular pay cheque coming in each month. The way to combat the insecurity is to plan ahead. Always have a range of jobs on the go, some done and awaiting payment, some commissioned and underway, and some which you are trying to 'sell' as ideas. You should also be constantly writing to new contacts asking for work.

Nevertheless, however carefully you plan ahead there will be times when you feel anxious about your finances. If you don't think you can cope with this sort of worry then maybe the freelance life isn't for you.

3   Dedication and Perseverance

You have to be prepared to stick at it, maybe for years, in the face of endless rejection. The one golden rule of being a successful writer is: NEVER GIVE UP.

4   Insight and Understanding

You need to look beyond the obvious and the superficial. You need to be able to see why things work and to assess what is important, to see links and patterns and draw conclusions.

5   Marketing and Sales Ability

You need to know what people want to buy, and then you need to be able to sell it to them. That means being able to write persuasive sales letters and talk convincingly on the telephone. It's a competitive market out there and you need to make your work stand out from the rest.

6   Boundless Curiosity

You must want to find out the answers to things. If you are not interested in the subject you are writing about you will never be able to interest your readers.

7   The Ability to Question and Listen

You must be able to ask questions, even if they seem impertinent, and then you must be able to listen to the answers. Few people are really good at listening, being too busy thinking about what they are going to say next, but there is no other way for a writer to get information.

THE DISADVANTAGES OF BEING A FREELANCE WRITER

Anyone who dreams of being a writer is going to have to overcome a number of obstacles along the way.

1 *Lack of Financial Security*

As I've already mentioned, however successful you are, you will never have what's known as a 'steady' income. Some months you may earn huge amounts and other months you may earn nothing. Some clients may pay late or not at all. You may never be able to predict for more than a few months ahead what your income is likely to be, although it's possible to reduce your level of insecurity by working for many different clients and planning ahead.

2 *Frequent Rejection*

Every writer has their work rejected more often than it is accepted. Even when an editor or publisher accepts something, they may still want to make major changes. As you become more experienced you will be able to raise the proportion of acceptances, but you will never reach 100 per cent. This is a healthy situation, but it is also hard to take when you have put so much love and care into your work. You have no choice but to accept it and keep going.

3 *Lack of Support*

When you work in a company you are nearly always part of a team. You have a boss you can go to for help, colleagues to moan with when things go wrong, and subordinates to blame. None of this support is there for the freelancer. If you are lucky you will have a supportive partner, but there are limits to how much you can call on them. Sometimes you will become part of a publishing team when you are producing a book, but as soon as the book is finished they will move on to other writers. A freelance writer is on their own most of the time.

4 *Domestic Distractions*

For some people the very idea of working at home is anathema. All they want to do is escape from their families, finding it impossible to get any work done if there are distractions around, or fearing that their marriages will crumble under the strain of too much togetherness. In some cases the demands of the family − particularly on mothers − are too great to allow for any writing work to be done in the home.

It's possible to solve such problems by taking an office or some shared office space but the rent will be an added expense, and you will have to allow for the time and cost involved in getting there.

5 *Public Indifference*

When you first start to sell articles or get your books published, you get very excited as publication day approaches. Your name is going to be up there on the cover, or at the top of the magazine page, for everyone to see. All your critics and doubters will be shamed by your success and all your supporters will throw their hats in the air and cheer.

After the initial euphoria of actually seeing your name there, the horrible truth will quickly dawn on you: hardly anyone notices the names of writers.

Ask anyone to name as many writers as they can, and they will come up with a few novelists − most of whom have been dead for years, if not centuries − and a couple of journalists who have been famous for decades and appear regularly on television.

There is such a vast amount of written material being pumped out by publishers and the media every day that few pieces of writing ever set the world alight. The chances are that even your own mother won't notice your triumph unless you tell her which issue of the magazine to buy, or send her down to the bookshop to order your latest tome.

Publication of anything is nearly always met by indifference from the rest of the world. If you are lucky, someone might write to the editor of the publication your piece appeared in to contradict some statement you made, or simply to say how awful they thought it was. Perhaps you will receive a few lukewarm reviews for a book.

The only way to handle such disappointments is just to climb back on to your steed of ambition and struggle on, turning your attention to the next book, the next article, the next screenplay.

These early difficulties are what make it possible to be successful later. Most of the people will be giving up at the first hurdles. Those who stay in the saddle end up with the field to themselves.

A FEW GOLDEN RULES OF FREELANCING

Never Mind the Art, Learn the Craft

Some readers may already be bristling with indignation at the superficiality of all that I have said so far. Perhaps they believe that writing is a noble calling, and writers should strive to reach ever greater heights of artistic endeavour, whether or not anyone buys their work. There is something in what they say – but not much.

Writing is a craft, and sometimes in practising your craft you may produce something so beautiful or eloquent that other people will find it has an emotional effect on them far beyond mere enjoyment or admiration of the skill involved. For those people, it is a work of art; for everyone else it is the product of fine craftsmanship. And if you intend to earn money from your writing you're likely to achieve much more success if you look on it as a craft. Find out what you can sell and then create it, rather than the other way round.

Give Your Genius a Chance

If you become a freelance writer you may, in time, prove to be a creative genius. Even if you don't, you will still experience all the satisfactions I have already mentioned, as well as the hope that one day your genius will be recognised.

By establishing a reputation for yourself as a writer, building a network of contacts and practising your craft, you increase the chance that any genius hidden within you will be discovered. After all, unless you make yourself into a writer in the first place, how are you going to be able to create the masterpiece which stamps your name on all the history books?

Be Patient

Months or even years after an article of yours has appeared in print a friend may mention casually that they saw it, or another editor may ring you and ask you to write something else on the same theme, or the subject of a later interview may say they admired some other piece you did.

For every ten pieces you write, one may cause a little interest in some circles and so, very, very slowly, you begin to build a reputation. The rewards will never come as soon as you expect them – and by the time they do come you will probably have grown too world-weary, cynical and mercenary to be that impressed by them – but they will still be well worth having. Becoming better known will make it easier to sell new work, but success will not give you the same heady excitement that it would have done at the beginning of your career.

TRAINING AND FINANCES

Should You Do a Training Course?

The brief of this book is to tell people how to make money from their writing, not how to write. As far as I know, there is no training facility which covers this, although many of the newspaper advertisements for correspondence courses say they 'guarantee' to teach you to write material which sells.

When you are at the beginning of your career, anyone who can teach you anything should be listened to. Whether the advice is worth paying for is a decision that each person must make for themselves.

By the time you read this book you may have already taken your first steps into the profession, perhaps as a journalist on a local or trade paper. That will at least give you a body of work to show around, and a useful insight into how editors work and what they need from freelancers.

Alternatively, you may have been on a creative writing course, which may have resulted in you writing some specu-lative pieces. Again this will help you through the initial stages.

If you have done neither of these things, and neither is by any means a requirement of freelance success (in fact some might argue the opposite), then you must start writing in order to catch up. Every bit of training and experience comes in useful at some stage, but the only thing that really matters is that you start writing and try to sell the results.

The best way to train is to do it. If you can't persuade anyone to pay for your work immediately, start by practising and honing your craft, as an amateur. Depending on your situation, you could perhaps write a Christmas pantomime for the local school, produce a newsletter for a society, charity or your company, or contribute to a school or college newspaper.

Should You Give Up Your Day Job?

For many people starting out as freelancers, the biggest problem is that they can't afford to give up their day jobs. It is inconceivable that they could survive on the amounts of money they are likely to be able to generate in the early months and years, especially if they have dependants.

There are very few bank managers who would be willing to lend someone the money to finance a launch into the freelance writing market. They would, in fact, be very unwise to do so. It takes a long time to start generating the sort of money needed to pay interest rates as well as start-up costs and living expenses, and there are no guarantees at the beginning as to how soon you will be able to get the money in. (For more on the financial aspects of freelancing, see Chapter 20.)

Most people, therefore, have to start by fitting their writing activities in with their regular jobs, until the time comes when they know they can support themselves on writing alone and they can wave the boss goodbye. Alternatively they can look for 'earning jobs', which fit in with their writing ambitions.

If your ultimate aim is to be a writer, then you should take jobs which provide you with interesting material to write about, and do not demand so much time and energy that you never get round to pursuing your real dream. If they provide you with writing experience at the same time (as in public relations or publicity work), so much the better.

It is no good becoming a trainee manager at a major bank or manufacturing company. The career demands of those sorts of positions are simply too great. You would never have the mental energy left to write, let alone the time.

You would be better advised to take a variety of more menial jobs that would provide you with material to write about, and would probably provide fewer career comforts to distract you from your writing goal. In other words, you need to find jobs to finance your writing, not replace it.

Many would-be writers take on jobs along the way to pay the rent, but then find it easier to stay with those jobs rather than get back out and survive on their writings. If you don't really need the money, you may be tempted to write self-indulgently, and to continue editing and polishing work for years rather than risking rejection by sending it out. The possibility of hunger is a great motivator.

'But', I hear you cry, 'I thought this book was going to tell me how to make money from freelance writing, not how to stay out of the "money trap".'

Quite right, and in the long term you should be able to earn much more from writing – and have much more fun – than if you take a more conventionally 'secure' job. In the short term, however, you will have to make some financial sacrifices. Look on it as a sort of savings scheme for the future. You are building a skill and resource which will be enormously valuable to you later on, but it will take time.

What about older people who may not feel that they can afford to make these sacrifices? Well, it's true that someone who sets out to be a writer straight from school needs very little money to survive on, whereas someone who has already established a comfortable lifestyle is going to find the transition to the freelance life more painful. But IT'S NEVER TOO LATE.

Older people have some important advantages. Firstly, they are already proficient at some other profession or skill. This means that although they have to start by taking a drop in living standards, they do at least have a financial and knowledge base to start from. If they own a house, for instance, they may be trapped by large mortgage repayments, but at least they have some capital and something to sell if the worst comes to the worst.

21

SEPARATING THE DREAMERS FROM THE ACHIEVERS

Anyone who tells you they are a writer, but who hasn't actually sold any of their work yet, has not so far proved anything. They should be placed just a few notches above the sort of people who wander around singing Elvis Presley ballads into imaginary hand mikes.

How do you go from dreaming to achieving?

Step 1

Decide what your ultimate goals are. If you were able to travel anywhere you wanted, where would you go? If you could meet anyone you wanted, who would you choose? What sort of writing would you truly like to do? Once you know the answers to these questions, you can start thinking about practical ways of reaching your goals.

Step 2

Organise a comfortable working environment for yourself. It could just be a boxroom under the stairs to start with, or it might be a beach house in Malibu. Wherever it is, it must be somewhere where you can go and work whenever you feel like it, or whenever an opportunity presents itself.

Step 3

Decide what skills, disciplines and subjects will be useful to you in attaining your long-term goals. Then begin to find out about them with a view to sharing them with others as you go along, in your writing. The harder and more complex the subjects you choose, the more material you will have to write about.

The knowledge you gain could be useful to you in your personal life as well. You might, for instance, need to learn about painting and wallpapering in order to save money on decorators — do it and write about your experiences for others. You may simply be interested in an academic subject for its own sake – make sure you know everything there is to know about it and be aware of where it will lead you next.

Step 4

Find out about all the pros and cons of being self-employed. Learn about income tax, VAT and accounts (there are some useful business books listed in the Bibliography). Customs and Excise will be very helpful with VAT enquiries, and the Inland Revenue will provide you with guidelines for income tax. It's worth getting a reputable accountant to give you a rough outline of what your tax situation will be (see Chapter 21).

Prepare a business plan (see p. 203) which will focus your mind on what your product will be and who is likely to buy it. Talk to all the other self-employed people you know to find out what the potential pitfalls are.

Step 5

Be sure in your own mind that you really feel the need to communicate your thoughts, feelings and discoveries to others. Without that drive it will be hard to keep going during the difficult times.

Step 6

Start writing.

2

Starting Out

The first thing you need, as I've already said, is a comfortable working environment. If you choose to work from home you won't need a great deal of space but you will need a reasonable amount of peace and quiet. For the sake of your long-term health, it's worth finding a comfortable chair and a desk at the right height. Make sure, as well, that you have enough light.

If you can't work at home, and you have to get an office, it should be as near as possible, so that you don't have to waste time travelling.

At this early stage you need to keep outgoings to a minimum. Unless it is absolutely unavoidable, I'd advise you not to spend money on renting offices. It is always going to be more expensive than you expect, since you not only have to find the rent, you also have to pay the expenses and upkeep for things like lighting, heating, telephones, cleaning and repairs, not to mention the costs of travelling to and from the premises. This is all money which you should be keeping for yourself.

THE TOOLS OF THE TRADE

Some of the following 'tools of the trade' are essential, and others will just make your life easier.

24

Reference Books

Most writers need to have a basic grounding in grammar, spelling and punctuation, but they certainly don't have to have a degree in English literature from Oxford. Indeed, too high a level of literary education might even be a hindrance, resulting in a tendency towards introspection rather than action.

There are dictionaries to help with spelling, and plenty of textbooks to help with grammar. A thesaurus will also provide a useful source of alternative words when you find you are repeating yourself. However you need to make sure that you don't start using unnaturally grand-sounding words – the result will be artificial at best and pretentious at worst.

Many people who feel unable to write grammatically are really suffering from a lack of self-confidence. Most of us talk grammatically – albeit colloquially. It is not a huge step to move from an acceptable level of spoken grammar to an acceptable level of written grammar. I am certain that I learned less about grammar from my English teacher than I did from having my parents correct the way I spoke at home.

After their dictionary and thesaurus, the most vital books for a freelancer are the *Writers' and Artists' Yearbook* (see Bibliography) and whichever directory or media guide (see Useful Addresses) is most relevant to their field.

Typing Skills

If you only ever learn one skill, typing will be the most useful to you as a writer. You can easily teach yourself to type from one of the many typing books available, or you can take a course at any secretarial college.

All professional writers are expected to produce typed copy. So if you can't type you're going to have to pay other people to do it for you – and you won't be able to afford that at the beginning. You will also miss out on the many advantages of word-processing (see p. 27) and desktop publishing.

In addition, when times are hard you will be able to take on typing work for other people in order to earn some money.

Presentation Skills

The first judgements about your work will be based on your standards of presentation. There are plenty of books on the market to tell you how to lay material out (see Bibliography) but the basic rules are to make it as neat, clean and easy to read as possible.

Articles and manuscripts should be typed with wide margins and double spacing. The pages should only ever be printed on one side; they must always be numbered, in case someone drops the lot on the floor; and it is better if you don't carry a paragraph on from one page to the next.

If you have a word-processor you can set it up to do all these things automatically, and you need never think about them again.

If you are unsure about how to lay out business letters, consult one of the books listed in the Bibliography. If you send amateurish-looking letters to potential clients they will assume that you are an amateurish writer and won't use you.

The golden rule is brevity. No business letter should be more than one page long. It should explain why you are writing and what you are suggesting or asking for, and it should ask for a response. Nothing else.

It should always be typed (single spaced) and addressed correctly to the relevant decision-maker — by name not just job title.

Editing letters down to the bare essentials is a good exercise for any writer. If you send out bad letters no one is going to believe that you can write anything else.

Shorthand Skills

Unless you are writing fiction, learning shorthand will give you a definite advantage. It is possible to get by with a sort of scrawled speedwriting, but the more accurate your skills the more easily you will be able to decipher your notes and write them up into articles.

Whenever you are interviewing someone, there will always be bits that you forget unless you record them in some way. The more information someone is giving you, the harder it is to keep up with them.

You can record them, literally, on a tape-recorder, but that means having to listen to the whole tape again when you come to write the piece. If you can get the information down on a shorthand pad you will be able to skim through it weeks later, recall everything that was said, and select the most useful items for your first draft.

Word-processors

If there is any way you can get your hands on a word-processor right at the beginning of your career, then do it. Any IBM compatible PC will be fine (Apple Macs are also a possibility). The advantage of IBM compatible models is the disks are compatible with most publishers' systems. It is important to have a good laser printer. Access to the Internet and e-mail can be useful and may soon be essential for people wanting to appear successful and businesslike. To have a facility for a modem linking the computer to the telephone would be a wise precaution for the future and costs very little.

When word-processors first came on to the market many writers claimed that they would never use them, that it was unnatural to write on screen, and that they would stick to their trusty old typewriters. I daresay they said the same about electric typewriters when they first came out, and manual ones before that. They probably said the same about fountain pens when they didn't want to give up using their quills.

It's all nonsense. It is the quality of the ideas that is important, not the method of recording and communicating them. The more efficient and labour-saving the method is, the better for the writer and the product. If you have learnt how to type on an ordinary typewriter it will only take a few hours to master a word-processor, and from then on you will be able to do in two hours what would take you eight hours on an electric typewriter.

With a word-processor you need never spend time retyping anything. You can move text around, insert new bits of information, delete repetition and generally polish it up to the best of your ability. You will most need the services of such a

27

faithful and uncomplaining servant at the beginning of your career, when you will probably have to work very hard and produce several versions of each piece of work.

In summary, go to your bank manager on your knees if you have to, but get access to a word-processor as soon as possible. If you truly don't feel you can afford one, then a decent electric typewriter will provide a sufficiently high standard of presentation. It will simply mean that you have to work a great deal harder to achieve the same results. (Don't forget that other freelancers, with whom you are competing, will have word-processors.)

Telephones

The telephone is a vital tool. Sitting at home you can interview twenty people in a day (provided they are all available) on the phone. If you had to go and meet all of them personally you might be able to fit four in during a working day, but even that would be a rush. You would probably only manage two.

Since you will be spending so much time on the phone, it's worth investing in a good one. Cordless ones are particularly convenient, giving you the freedom to move about the house, which can be useful if you have to look things up, want to sit in the garden, let a barking dog out while talking, or escape from a room full of fighting children without interrupting the conversation.

Automatic dialling facilities are also useful as a time-saver, as are loudspeaker systems for hands-off conversations (although the sound quality is usually not good enough for actually doing interviews).

A mobile phone will be useful if you spend a lot of time on the road, but since you generally need to be writing at a desk while you listen, their usefulness is limited.

None of these things are essential at first, however. When I started twenty years ago I was sharing a pay phone in a London flat with a dozen other people.

Answerphones

Having said that, a reliable answerphone is *vital*. People do not expect to have to keep calling back just because you are out, particularly if they are the ones giving you the work.

All too often when you have to do a number of interviews, people will be out or unable to talk when you call, and you will have to leave messages for them to ring you back. If you don't have an answering machine you then have to stay in all day waiting for their calls. And it is a fundamental rule of nature that 'calls you stay in for never come'. They always come just as you step outside the front door.

Although the telephone is an essential tool you should beware of using it as an excuse to stay in an ivory tower, away from the real world. Sometimes it is worth taking the time to meet someone personally, just to get a broader picture.

Fax Machines

Fax machines can greatly assist a freelance writer in getting briefs quickly, and in turning articles around virtually immediately. An editor can fax you a brief in the morning, you can write the article during the day and fax it back in the evening. Before faxes you would have had to use the post (which could have taken a week to go both ways), a motorbike messenger which would have cost a fortune, or you would have dictated the piece down the phone (which was only really possible on a national newspaper, and was always immensely time-consuming and prone to inaccuracy).

Faxes also double as simple copying machines and are a convenience verging on a necessity. Most clients would expect a freelance to have a fax, although it can be attached to the normal phone line and need not have a dedicated line, unless you are using it so much the line is being blocked. The best ones are combined with answering machines and cost a few hundred pounds. If your start-up budget really won't stretch to that you can come to an arrangement with a local fax bureau, using their facilities for both sending and receiving and only paying for the services you use. The amount of time that will take up, however, will probably make it a false economy.

Tape-Recorders

Using a tape-recorder as well as taking notes is like wearing a belt with braces, but it is worth doing. If a conversation is going well, you may want to stop taking notes for a while in order to keep the flow going – you can only do that if you know the recorder is still running.

The smaller and more portable a tape-recorder is, the better. Many interviewees are still unnerved by them. Consequently you need a machine which is reliable and simple to operate, so you won't have to keep fiddling with it and reminding your interviewee of its existence. Always check the sound level beforehand, and carry spare batteries with you, changing them well before they are due to run out.

When it comes to playing the tape back in the privacy of your office, you may need a slightly larger machine with better sound quality – probably one that runs off the mains. There are several suitable tape-recorders on the market, none of them very expensive.

Stationery

Presentation is always important in business, and the first step is to have some good headed notepaper printed. Any high street printer can do it for you. Most of them will make design suggestions as well, if you haven't got any ideas of your own. It's best to choose one you like and ask them to copy it.

It's worth taking some trouble over the design because it is likely to have to last you for some time. Rather like choosing a wallpaper for your sitting room, you want something which isn't too startling, so that you will be able to live with it for a number of years. It is much cheaper to have more paper printed with the same design than to ask the printer to change it each time.

The paper should be A4 in size, and must have your address and telephone number on it (and fax number if you have one). You will also need envelopes for sending letters, and envelopes big enough to take articles.

Business cards and compliment slips are also useful, and don't cost much if you use the same design as the notepaper.

They last for years and you will find you usually only have to renew them when you move house.

Fortunately, a good headed paper is the only sort of image-building material you are going to have to invest in at the beginning. Pity the poor person running a small business who has to invest in brochures, signs for outside the office or factory, packaging, invoices and all the rest.

Your notepaper will be introducing you to the market, telling it that you are in business, that you are serious about what you are doing, and likely to be around in a few months time. It can also be used for invoicing.

THE LESSONS TO LEARN

Once you've set yourself up with a place to work and the basic tools of your trade you're almost ready to begin. But just before you take the plunge I'd like to share some of the most important lessons I've learnt as a freelance writer.

1 *Always Plan Ahead*

As I've already mentioned, a freelancer needs to combat insecurity by having several jobs on the go, at different stages of completion. If you have a number of irons in the fire you will never be completely out of work, and you will have a rough idea of how much money will be coming in over the next few months. You can then plan accordingly – perhaps by taking in typing work, doing a part-time job or simply cutting down on your spending until things get better.

A successful freelancer is making new contacts all the time. If one magazine stops using them or closes down, they go out looking for another. They are able to take evasive action as soon as trouble seems to be looming on the horizon.

As a freelancer, you also need to plan ahead in case of illness or disability. There are a number of insurance policies you can take out to cover yourself and it's worth choosing carefully.

The most common type of policy guarantees you a certain income if you are unable to work, due to illness or injury. You can choose how high that income needs to be in order for you to survive, while making sure that the payments are affordable. Most of the plans do not start paying out until three months after your incapacity starts. However, if you have been in business for any length of time, money you are owed will continue to come in during that three-month period, so you should be able to stay afloat.

There are also a number of policies which cover you for a stay in hospital. For further information ask at your bank, or ask an insurance broker or independent financial adviser to let you have a selection of options from the major insurance companies.

2 *Study Potential Outlets*

Many people, when considering a writing career, have a particular outlet in mind for their work − probably a type of publication which they themselves enjoy as consumers. In fact all media provide potential markets for your work. You might be able to write for anything from films to television, radio to live theatre, political and business speeches to comedy routines, company brochures to press releases. All these media, and many others, involve professional writers, and could provide you with sources of income.

Read everything you can get your hands on, firstly to learn about the world, secondly to give you ideas for new markets for your work, and thirdly to become familiar with a wide range of literary styles which you can adapt for your own use. That doesn't only mean reading Proust or Shakespeare − although any of the literary classics will be useful − but everything that comes your way, from trade magazines to romantic fiction, from literary prize-winners to airport blockbusters, from direct mail items that land on your doormat to the cookery books lurking in your kitchen.

The printed word will give you access to worlds you may never have experienced personally, but which you need to understand. Drink it all in. Everything you collect will come in useful at some stage.

3   *Prepare Yourself to Deal with Rejection*

You will have to get used to being rejected, and you need to have this clearly in mind before you start trying to sell your work. If you are going to be so hurt by rejection that you won't be able to work effectively, then you will have to find another way to earn a living because there is simply no way round it. At the beginning of your career virtually everything you do will be rejected, often with no explanation at all. There is no way of avoiding this unless you are extremely lucky and fall into a specialist niche immediately.

> If ten per cent of your output sells you are doing well; if one per cent sells you are still in business.

It usually happens the same way:

You have what seems to you a brilliant idea.

You write it in a glow of excitement.

You send it off in the certainty that it will be accepted.

You wait – sometimes months.

You begin to plan what you will do with the money, and what pictures you will suggest they use, and what you will order for lunch when the editor concerned invites you out to a restaurant to discuss other articles.

It finally arrives back on the doormat with a printed slip enclosed. Or, worse still, you can't stand the wait any longer so you ring up to enquire if they are planning to use the piece. They can't even remember receiving it and politely decline your offer to send another copy.

This is going to happen to you over and over and over again.

I might even venture to suggest that if you aren't getting rejected then you aren't trying out enough new or challenging ideas. It is the people who stretch themselves beyond their known limits who get rejected most often. But that doesn't make it any easier to bear at the beginning, when your self-confidence is low anyway.

4   *Develop a Philosophy*

You therefore have to develop a philosophy which will help to

33

raise your spirits after these blows to your pride, and keep you toiling away at the next project.

Try this. Go into a major bookshop or newsagent and just stand there staring at the massive numbers of books and magazines on display. Then tell yourself that this is but the tiniest tip of the iceberg. Most of the books published each week aren't on the shelves because there isn't room for all of them; the magazines only live for a week or a month before being replaced by new issues; and the majority of special interest magazines don't get into the newsagents at all.

Somebody has had to write all this stuff, so you know there is a market for the service you are offering. It is also unlikely that all the people who are getting their work published are that much brighter than you. You know, therefore, that it is possible to make a living as a professional writer.

Hold on to that thought for a moment.

In order to get to that position, however, you have got to learn how the business works, what people will and won't publish, what will make money and what won't. The only way you can learn all this is by trying everything and seeing what works.

So try to look upon each rejection as another brick in the wall of your experience. Each time something comes back you have learnt something new about the writing business, and you have added to your store of knowledge and experience. Keep reading all the stories about how publishers rejected *Day of the Jackal* and *Watership Down* and all the others, and just have faith that you will get there too in the end.

If there is one quality that a professional freelance writer needs above all others it is perseverance. However many times you are knocked back at the beginning, just keep going. You may not break through to a level of achievement which you find acceptable for years – but never give up.

The only sure way of failing is to give up trying. Would you rather achieve your goals in five or ten years' time or not at all? The choice is yours.

In the meantime, make sure that you do each piece of work as well as you possibly can. And hold on to the belief that this could be the one which gets you started, or gets you to the next stage.

34

5 *Forget It As Soon As You Finish It*

Once you have finished the work, send it off and start on something else immediately. Like a watched kettle, a waited-for acceptance will never arrive. Only chase up the first project if you haven't heard anything for several weeks and if you have someone else lined up to send it to.

By the time it comes back you should have sent at least one other piece of work out, preferably several, and you will be able to transfer your hopes on to the new projects. Because you have moved on in this way, you will be less emotionally involved with the piece which has been rejected. You may even be able to read it more objectively than before and see ways in which it can be improved.

When it comes back, read the rejected work again and, if you truly believe it is up to the required professional standards, send it out to someone else immediately. Always be working on something new. Never pin your hopes on something you are waiting to hear about.

Every time you sell something or get into print, use that achievement as a stepping stone to the next. If you have had an article published in a magazine, send copies of it to other editors who need to know your track record. Every time you achieve any sort of goal, immediately go for something bigger.

6 *Understand the Product You are Selling*

The only way to get other people to pay you money is to provide them with a product or service that they need or desire. Writing is no exception to this rule. So, before you can achieve anything, you have to ask yourself: 'What am I selling?'

Your first answer might be that you are selling words on paper – WRONG. The words you commit to paper are merely the tools you use to package and distribute your real product. They are just one stage in your production process.

What you are really selling is ideas, information and/or entertainment. You are either selling your own ideas and experiences or you are re-packaging and selling-on those of other people.

The final form of your product may have nothing to do with the written word. It might, for instance, be a movie based on your original idea or on your script. It could be a speech or lecture which you wrote for a politician or businessman, or it could be words spoken on a video or audio tape. It might simply be pictures, filmed in a way you have suggested.

Always remember that you are selling your understanding and interpretation of the world around you, and your ability to communicate these things to other people. Once you have understood that fundamental fact, you will begin to see a thousand different ways in which you can adapt and package your skills in order to earn money.

3

Where Do You Begin?

So here you are: no experience, no track record, no contacts. And you need to convince a bunch of highly experienced, professional editors and publishers that you are a competent and reliable writer, and that they should buy something from you.

Don't worry − it can only get better.

There are two things you need to get the ball rolling:

1   You have to write something which you can start trying to sell, and which you can show to people who want to see an example of your style.
2   You can start to contact people who you think might commission articles from you despite the fact that you are only just setting out. Not many will, but you only need one in order to start. There is no other way to become a freelance writer than to JUST START DOING IT.

WHAT SHOULD YOU WRITE ABOUT?

You should write about what interests you − something you either know a lot about already, or which you would like to know more about. You should, in other words, write the sort of material you would like to read.

If you already have a skill or a job which has given you experience of a subject other people will want to know about, then you have a head start. For instance, if you have been working as an accountant, a doctor or a solicitor you will know what sort of problems people usually seek expert advice on. You will therefore be able to write about your subject in a useful and saleable way. Similarly, if you service cars, undertake do-it-yourself projects, knit jumpers or make curtains, you have a skill which you can write about, and which you can research further.

Start by sitting down and making two lists:

1   What do I know about?
2   What do I want to find out about?

Don't be modest − once you start listing things you may be surprised by how many there are. How many of the following, for instance, do you know enough about to write an article?

Cooking, cocktail-making, travel, car maintenance, carpentry, gardening, roof insulation, child-care, photography, pottery, hiking, golf, building an extension, accountancy, law, sewing, knitting, flower-arranging, book-binding, charity work, music, exercise, diet, health-care, tree surgery, picture-framing, skiing, buying a house, getting married, getting divorced, coping with illness, hairdressing, going for job interviews, yoga, tennis, shopping, dining out, buying wine, training horses, breeding dogs or tropical fish, skate-boarding, wind-surfing, fishing, shooting, dog-racing, computing, retailing, fashion, catering, cleaning, watching television, making home videos, laying a patio, replacing windows, arranging a party, dating, dealing with acne, premenstrual tension, impotence, stress . . .

The list could go on for ever because people are interested in an infinite number of subjects. Anything that other people want to know more about is going to produce material for articles, books or radio and television programmes.

Some writers tend to lock themselves away in ivory towers. Sooner or later they run out of new ideas and experiences to write about, and their work becomes repetitive, derivative and uninteresting. A few established writers can get away with it because they have found a formula which works, and which they can keep on repeating – but not many. Some end up writing books about writers writing books about writers . . .

Stay in touch with real life. Do as much eavesdropping as you can. Two girls talking about boyfriend problems on a bus, a group of businesspeople arguing in a restaurant, a bunch of drunken youths in a pub, or a man on a soap box proclaiming his theological beliefs: they will all feed your imagination and your understanding of the human condition.

These people also make up your ultimate audience. They are the ones who buy books, newspapers and magazines, watch television, listen to the radio and buy tickets to the movies. They are the ones the businesspeople and politicians want to influence, and the comedians and actors want to entertain. If you don't know what their interests are, how can you tailor your products to suit their needs?

WHO ARE YOU GOING TO SELL TO?

Having made your lists of subjects to write about, you can start to think about who you should approach with your ideas.

Many people will start by writing articles for magazines and newspapers. They are easier to write than books or scripts because they are shorter. They are also easier to sell because magazines and newspapers are being printed all the time and their pages have to be filled.

In the last twenty years there has been a media explosion in this area. There are now several competing titles on virtually every subject you can think of, and a lot on areas you never even knew existed.

You will already know about some of the publications you want to get into, since they cover your own areas of special interest. If you are keen on knitting, for instance, you will know which magazines carry articles on knitting, or DIY, or car maintenance, or skiing, or financial planning, or whatever. You will, however, need a far bigger pool of potential customers than that if you are to succeed.

There are several ways of searching out potential customers:

1 *Look at What's on Sale*

Go down to your local newsagent and browse through the shelves to see what else is selling. Buy the relevant publications and take them home for closer study.

You should also look at books on your subject, read as many of them as possible, and make a note of who the publishers are, so that you can approach them with ideas for books later on. You may need to quote several experts, so the more material you have access to the better.

2 *Go Through the Reference Books*

Remember that what you see on the newsagents' shelves is only the tip of the iceberg — far more magazines are distributed direct to subscribers or potential readers through the post. You need to find out everything else that could possibly provide you with an outlet for your work.

A number of reference books, which are updated regularly, list all the publications available. You may find some of them in your local library. Check the Useful Addresses section of this book for the names of helpful writers' magazines and journals. The more publications you read in related fields, the better.

Initially, all you need is the name of the magazine, the address for sending editorial copy to, and the telephone number. You can then phone and ask for the name of the overall editor, or the editor for the section you are interested in.

Making an exploratory phone call can be very daunting, but it is never as hard as you think. You don't even have to give your name in many cases and your query will be answered by the telephonist or receptionist.

As soon as someone answers you just have to say, 'Hello, I

want to send in an article on ... Who should I address it to?'

Usually it's as simple as that. Sometimes the telephonist will put you through to someone else and you will just have to repeat the question. Occasionally they won't give the person's name – they will just tell you to address it to 'the editor'. Ask if you can have their name; if they refuse you will have to assume it is their company policy.

A small magazine will just have an editor and possibly an assistant. A slightly larger one may have a features editor and a news editor. National magazines and newspapers will have cookery editors, women's editors, beauty editors, sports editors, and so on. Not all these people will work in the magazine's office all the time. Some of them will also be free-lancers, sending their material in. You will still be able to contact them at the addresses given in the publications, if not by phone.

Whenever possible you should address your letter to someone by name, and you must know how to spell the name correctly. If you have a copy of the publication you will usually find this information printed somewhere around the contents page.

3 Check the Directories and Media Guides

Some of the better directories and media guides (see Useful Addresses) are produced for the public relations industry. They list the magazine editors and other editorial staff, and update their information every month or so. Because they are designed for a business market, and are being continuously updated, they are expensive and might not be a good investment until you have started to generate some income. To start with, you will have to rely on whatever books you can find at the local library, and your own research.

Even if you have found the name of the editor in a reference book or directory, it is worth ringing to check it. They do move around quite frequently and the books are sometimes out of date before they are published. That way you can also check the spelling of the name, the exact title (sometimes the people you want are called executive editors or features editors), and the address.

If at all possible, you should get copies of all the publications that end up on your list. In some cases this may only be possible by taking out subscriptions, which would be rather expensive. If, however, you are going to telephone to find out the name of the editor, you could ask at the same time how you can get hold of a copy of the magazine. People are usually very helpful when asked direct questions – but don't expect them to send you a free copy because they won't.

4 *Make Your List Even Bigger*

The bigger your list of potential customers the better. If you only have one target editor your chances of success are very slim; if you have ten people to approach you may well score one hit; if you have a hundred you could be in business before you know it.

You need to think laterally. Don't just list the magazines which are directly involved in your field. For instance, if your area of expertise is accountancy, don't limit yourself to the accountancy magazines. If you stick to the most specialised trade press you will be competing with experienced people from your own field, some of whom may know more about the subject than you do. These magazines also tend to have people on their staff who can provide much of the material you are offering – so why should they pay you?

Likewise, if knitting is your subject, you shouldn't just go to knitting magazines, nor should fishermen always send articles to the fishing titles, because that is what everyone else is doing.

The obvious titles should certainly be on your list because they are good potential customers, but they should only be a part of it. By finding the right angle or slant, you should be able to aim your product at a number of different outlets. For instance, the accountancy writer should approach every magazine where the readership might need accountancy advice. Just about every business in the world has to deal with accounts systems, tax inspectors, cashflow and interest rates. They all need advice and help and if you angle a story the right way you can make it relevant to them.

An article on accountancy might be of interest to general

management magazines, or to local newspapers, or specific trade magazines. A magazine read by freelance writers, for instance, might be interested in an article on how to deal with the tax authorities; a newspaper might be interested in an accountant's view of how to organise your personal finances, when to have children for maximum tax advantage, whether to buy or lease a car, and so on.

The knitting writer might be able to sell articles to any women's interest or fashion magazine, or any crafts and country pursuits journal. But they could also write about the knitting business (from shearing sheep to retailing the wool) for business and farming publications. There could be stories on dyeing wool, recycling old garments and any number of other angles.

Articles on DIY could be of interest to local papers — how to lag your pipes in the winter, how to build a conservatory in the summer, how to build a fireplace or barbecue. The same subjects, angled towards home-makers, could also be of interest to women's magazines, or home and garden journals.

Spend as much time as you need with the reference books and directories, thinking of ways in which your subject could be adapted to suit various different types of publication.

WHAT DO YOU DO NEXT?

You've decided what subjects you want to write about, and you've compiled a good long list of potential customers. Now how are you going to get them to publish your work?

1 *Test Your Ideas*

Look at each of your ideas and ask yourself some brutal questions:

- Will I be telling people something they don't know?
- Is it topical? Does it relate to something which is currently uppermost in people's minds?
- Will it help them to be happier, healthier, richer or better in any way?

If you can't say 'yes' to any of these questions, you probably haven't got a story, and you should move on to another idea.

2 *Write a Synopsis*

Once you're sure that you have a story, you need to write a synopsis, a summary of what the article is about. You could also include details of why you think it will interest the readers of that particular magazine, and why you are the best person to write it.

This synopsis has to give the editor confidence in your writing abilities. It must, therefore, be neatly presented, well written and sensibly structured. It must not ramble. It could be in the form of a letter or a sheet attached to a covering letter. A synopsis for an article should never take up more than one side of A4 paper. Let's look at a few examples.

Mr Smith starts off by writing to the editor of his local paper:

Dear Mr Bloggs,

SAVING THE LIVES OF LOCAL PEOPLE

I am a freelance writer specialising in home improvement subjects. As we are approaching winter again I wondered if you would be interested in an article on how the elderly can keep warm and save money at the same time.

The article would look at ways to stop draughts around doors and windows; how to keep heat from escaping through glass and through ceilings; and how to keep your feet warmer by covering draughty floors.

It would also contain advice on how to make sure that heating systems are operating efficiently and pipes don't freeze up.

Do you think this would be of interest to your readers?

Your sincerely,

John Smith

He might also write to the features editor of the national tabloid papers:

Dear Mr Bloggs,

OLD PEOPLE DYING

Last winter 3,000 old people died in this country as a direct result of inadequate insulation. There are five basic steps every householder can take which would have saved many of those lives.

I am a freelance writer specialising in home improvement subjects, and I would like to submit an article which outlines these five steps.

Is this something that would interest your readers?

Yours sincerely

John Smith

And to a homes and decor type magazine:

Dear Mr Bloggs,

MAKING A ROOM COSY AND SAVING MONEY

Nothing is more tempting than a warm room on a cold winter's evening, yet many people who live in old houses put up with draughts and high heating bills simply because they don't know how easy it is to transform such a room by following a few basic steps.

I am a freelance writer specialising in this area, and I wondered if you would be interested in an article on how to make a room 100 per cent warmer without spoiling its appearance.

Do you think this is something which would interest your readers?

Yours sincerely,

John Smith

3 *Send Out Your Letters*

Don't worry if you can only think of one or two really good angles – that's all you need to start with. And if the idea is topical and you need to make a quick sale, send the same idea to several editors at once. The odds are that only one of them will respond positively, and even then they may ask for a slightly different angle to the one you have suggested. If several rival editors want the same piece you have a problem. But it is a very nice problem to have, and very unusual for a beginner.

If more than one editor wants the article you will then have to decide which one to give it to. That may be decided by the tone of their response. Some will say definitely 'yes' and give you a deadline and a price, while others might say they will 'consider the piece if you would like to send it in'. In that case you should obviously start with the first one. Then if they end up not liking the resulting article, you can send it to the second.

If two editors give you a definite 'yes', you will have to base your decision on the relative prestige of the magazines and how much they are offering to pay. If there is direct competition then take up the best offer and be honest with the other one. (I have to say that this situation has never happened to me in twenty years, so I wouldn't lose too much sleep over it!)

Provided the article is not topical, it's best to have different angles for each magazine, or send each angle to one editor at a time.

4 *Keep a Record and Then Follow Up*

Keep a record of who you send what to, and when. You will be surprised at how quickly the rejections and re-submissions start piling up, and if you are sending out half a dozen different ideas in rotation to a list of twenty or thirty editors, it won't be long before you lose track of who has had what.

You need to make sure that you don't send them the same angle twice and you need to follow up with a phone call if you don't receive a response through the post.

A week after sending the letter, ring up and ask politely if they have received it and if they would be interested in seeing the article when it is written. It is quite possible that they will have forgotten all about your letter, and you will have to remind them of what it said. They will then make a decision over the phone. Once you have sold a few articles to an editor, and have built up the relationship to a point where they recognise your name when you ring up, you can begin to suggest ideas over the phone.

This will speed the process up considerably, allowing you to find out if an idea is a goer within a few minutes. Before you make the call, however, write down what the article will be about, with the main selling points, so that you can put the case swiftly and succinctly and not waste their time with waffle.

If they say 'no', accept it as final and don't try to argue with them. You could, however, just ask if there is anything else you could do for them. If they say 'no' again, leave them alone until you have another idea to offer them.

The moment you have a 'no' you can send the idea off to the next person on the list, and try to think of something else to offer the person who has just turned you down. The objective is constantly to remind them of your existence and of your willingness to do whatever they need, but not to pester them.

5 *Write the Piece Anyway*

While you are continuing this hunt for customers, you should be writing the articles anyway. There are a number of reasons for doing this:

- You need the experience and the practice.
- You need the information in order to sound authoritative when selling the idea.
- While doing the research you may stumble across other angles and ideas which you could be selling at the same time.
- An editor might say 'yes' but demand to have the article immediately. You need to be prepared.
- Once you have written something you will have a definite product to sell rather than just an idea for one.

47

6 *If They Say Yes ...*

There are two types of 'yes' at this stage. They may be saying 'Yes, the idea is good. We are willing to look at the article if you would like to send it.' They may still reject it for whatever reason, but at least you are one step further on.

Alternatively they may be saying, 'Yes, we will commission the article', in which case you need to know a number of things:

- How many words do they want? (1,000 to 1,500 would be typical)
- When is the deadline?
- How much do they pay?
- What do they want to do about pictures?

Make sure that you have fully understood which kind of 'yes' it is. If you are not sure and don't want to ask, assume it is the former until you have had a formal acceptance.

Some people, like certain professional writers' associations or unions, will tell you that there are minimum rates of pay, below which you shouldn't go. They will also say that you should have formal commissioning letters, and that the editors should agree to pay a rejection fee if they end up not using the article.

If you start insisting on all that, I'm afraid you are not going to get much further. At this stage in your career you need the editors more than they need you. They will have a standard rate for the job, and – when you are starting out – it is more important for you to get your work published than to get paid.

You can, however, ask if they would be prepared to pay expenses on top of the fee. This doesn't mean the cost of paper and typewriter ribbons, but could include travel expenses, large telephone bills and so on. If they say 'no', don't pursue it.

Some of them might send you an official commissioning letter – but not many will have the time – and if asked I would suggest you say you don't need one. You do, after all, need to build up a relationship of mutual trust with these people. Occasionally they will let you down, but not very often.

If you think a misunderstanding could arise at a later date, drop them a confirming letter, just outlining what you have agreed to do, when they can expect to receive it, and how much the agreed fee is.

If you mention a rejection fee the editor will think you are unsure that you can come up with the goods. DON'T DO IT. Assume they are going to love whatever you send them. If, for any reason, they don't, it is probably because you haven't done it well enough. If you do a good job and they don't use the article, you can sell it to a rival magazine later on.

Without making them think you don't know how to approach the subject, ask if there are any angles they particularly want covered, and anyone they would especially like you to quote in the article. The more closely you tailor the article to their requirements, the more likely they are to use you again. You also need as many leads as possible to make the piece as thorough as you can.

Ask them if they would like you to arrange photographs. (Make it clear that you are offering to take them yourself and will be charging for them, or that you will just be asking people if they have any shots of themselves which you can use.)

7 *Master Their Style*

Make sure you have a copy of the magazine you are writing for. If you can get in to meet the editor personally, so much the better for the sake of building up a long-term relationship. If they don't have time to see you, don't insist. Equally, if they are based at the other end of the country a visit would be impractical.

Read the magazine carefully and try to see what sort of style they like:

- Do they use a lot of quotes?
- Do they like long sentences and paragraphs, or do they like everything short and snappy?
- Do they assume a certain level of knowledge amongst their readers, or do they explain everything in detail?

Every medium is different. A quality newspaper has a very different style to a tabloid, and most publications have their own way of talking to their readers. You will not be able to get it exactly right for all of them. But they will expect you to get reasonably close so that they can edit and adjust what you have done without too much effort.

The more trouble you take at this stage, the more likely it is that you will get it right first time. This will not only save you time on re-writing; it will also make them keener to use you again.

8 *When You've Written the Article*

You may decide that you can't do your idea justice in a synopsis, and so you want to write the whole thing before you try to sell it. Or you may have been unable to interest anyone in the synopsis but you still think it is a good idea, so you have written it anyway.

For whatever reason, you now have an article, which you can send to potential customers. Start by sending it to anyone who may have shown the slightest glimmer of interest in the synopsis (if you sent one), and then move on through your list, only missing out people who definitely said they would not be interested.

Send the article with a covering letter and a stamped addressed envelope. If you have a word-processor you won't actually need the article back because you can always print out another copy, but it is still polite to send an SAE. If they are definitely not interested it will encourage them to reply quickly.

Having sent the article, give them a week before ringing to check if they are interested. If they aren't, then immediately print out a clean copy and send it to the next person on the list.

While talking to them, do not miss the opportunity to ask if there is anything else you might be able to do for them. If you have time, re-read the article each time it comes back, to see if it has become outdated or if you are able to improve it in any way before sending it out again.

If you get to the bottom of the list and no one has taken it, don't throw the article away. Keep it on file. It is raw material which you may well be able to rework and re-sell at a later date.

Keep a note of anything relevant which any of the editors say or write to you. You need to build up an accurate picture of their likes and dislikes, needs and problems. The clearer this picture, the more likely it is that you will be able to satisfy their needs at a later date.

9 *If Your Work is Rejected* . . .

It is very hard, when you are not all that confident about whether you can be a writer at all, to be told that a piece over which you have lavished hours or even days of loving care and attention is 'not quite what we are looking for'.

When it does happen there is a strong temptation to argue. DON'T! They are the customers and you have to give them what they want. If they aren't satisfied, you have failed and you must try again.

Alternatively, there is a temptation to give up and slink away to lick your wounds in private. DON'T! You can't become a professional writer unless you can satisfy your customers.

Ask them to explain why it is wrong, and do everything you can to put it right. You will always learn something from any criticism – much more, in fact, than if they say nothing and rewrite your article themselves. Going that way might save you some time and bother, but it will teach you nothing and will not encourage the editors to use you again. Show how eager you are to learn and to get it right, and ask them to tell you where you are going wrong.

Once you start researching, if it turns out that there just isn't a story there, admit it straight away rather than trying to fob them off with something half-baked. Ring them up and explain why you don't think you are going to be able to deliver, and ask if they have any ideas on how you can overcome the problem. Most of them will do their best to be helpful if they feel you are being honest with them.

4

Getting
Commissioned

There are two ways of getting work as a freelance writer. One is to generate ideas of your own and then sell them to prospective customers – which is largely what we have been talking about up till now. The second is for potential customers to approach you when they need material.

In order to do that they need to know:

- who you are
- how to contact you
- that you are reliable
- and that you understand their requirements.

This means that you need to market yourself (just like a plumber who needs to make his name known to potential customers so that it is his number they call when an emergency strikes).

How Do You Attract Potential Customers?

1 *Approach Existing Customers*

The major source of commissioned work for any freelancer will be previous satisfied customers. Whenever you send them material or contact them for any other reason you should therefore let them know that you are always in the market for more work. It just requires a simple sentence at the end of each letter or conversation: 'Is there anything else I can do for you?' or 'Let me know if you ever need material at short notice.'

2 Build a Network

Networking just means talking to people who know about the business you want to get into, and asking them who else you should be talking to. Make a list of people you could approach to ask for advice on freelance writing in general or on a specific area you want to specialise in. Other self-employed people, other writers, editors, publishers, television producers, or anyone remotely connected to the media, even if they can't help you themselves, might lead you on to other people who can.

You then ring them or write to them, making it clear that you are not asking for work or trying to sell them anything. You simply want to talk to them about the market and what sort of products you might be able to sell.

Some people will be too busy to talk to you, but some will be sufficiently flattered at being asked and will spare you some time.

When you go to see them, prepare your questions in advance and try to get some feedback on which areas they think will be most fruitful. Before you leave, ask them for the names of at least three other people you could talk to. Your first three contacts will thus lead to nine more, who will lead to twenty-seven more, who will lead to eighty-one more. Obviously it won't work as smoothly as that. But you can very quickly build up a network of contacts who know of you and your ambitions, and will recognise your name when you come back to them later with ideas and pieces of work.

3 Build Relationships

Every time you make a sale, whatever it is, you must try to turn it into another. Every one-off sale can lead to a steady stream of work, even if it is just an article sold through the post to an editor.

You could become a regular correspondent for a magazine or newspaper (doing everything by post, fax or phone) and never even meet the editor, though that would be unusual. In most cases you will need to build a relationship, which means getting in to see the editor at least once, and probably regularly.

It can be done on a formal basis, arranging to have lunch together occasionally, or going in to take briefs for articles. Or it can be done informally, with you delivering your articles in person rather than sending them.

If you can build and maintain a relationship in this way it will keep you at the forefront of an editor's mind and will encourage them to feel some sort of loyalty towards you. It could also mean that you are able to think up ideas together. An editor might mention a problem in conversation. It might never have occurred to him or her to approach you about it, but if you can suggest a solution you have strengthened the relationship by proving that you can solve their problems.

If you can build that sort of trust the editor may start ringing you and picking your brains even when they haven't yet worked out a clear brief for an article − they just know they need something to fill a certain space.

Once this starts happening, you need to be ready with some ideas. Ideally you need to be able to come up with something immediately, while their interest is still high. If that isn't possible, ask if you can call them back in an hour, or later the same day, to give yourself time to put together a list of possible ideas.

You may already have material in your files which you could update and adapt. This is the most profitable method, since it will probably only take you an hour or two to create an article instead of the usual day or two − but for the same money!

If you have nothing suitable in stock, you need to think quickly of anyone you have read about or talked to who might be a useful source of quotes. (You should always be adding to your collection of contact names and cuttings on subjects you are most often asked to write about. This will give you instant access to the latest developments and the names of people who are willing to be quoted on the subject.)

4 *Earn a Reputation as an Expert*

Some editors will approach you because you are known to be an expert in a particular subject. They, or their predecessors, may have used you before, or they may have read your work in other books or magazines, or they may simply know you because you have a high profile.

If they approach you on this basis you should be able to ask for rather more than the usual going rate, since they may be able to use your name and reputation to promote their product. A magazine which manages to persuade Norman Mailer to write about sex is likely to advertise the fact on the cover and possibly even boast about it in a wider marketing campaign. Likewise, a motoring magazine which gets the most famous racing driver of the day to test-drive a new car is going to broadcast the fact. They will expect to pay more because that person's name will help to sell more copies of the magazine.

Many freelance writers never achieve expert status, and others take many years to become known as an authority on a particular subject. Nevertheless, it's worth striving to build this sort of reputation because it will make it much easier to get work and it will make the work that much more profitable.

PUTTING YOUR MARKETING PLAN INTO ACTION

Direct Mail

This is almost certainly the most cost-effective and efficient method of reaching potential customers.

Just keep sending them letters containing suggestions and ideas for articles (or books, or films or television programmes – whatever it is they need).

If they have never bought anything from you before, include photocopies of articles you have written for similar publications. Whenever you have an article published, always take copies of it to send out to anyone who might possibly hire you. If you send an editor a huge pile of articles you have had published, they will probably only skim through one or two, but they will notice where they were published and will feel suitable reassured that you are a professional and reliable writer.

It's sometimes worth preparing a small brochure or promotional leaflet about yourself. I haven't listed brochures in Chapter 2 as 'tools of the trade' because they are not essential, may not always be appropriate and might be too expensive to produce until you are fairly well established.

If you do decide to get a brochure printed, it will give you an opportunity to list your relevant achievements without having to enclose a huge collection of samples. You want something that will catch the right people's attention, that they will be able to file easily, and that will demonstrate you are serious and professional in your approach. In addition, when you get your brochure updated, it will give you a reason to do a mass mailing to all potential customers.

Always enclose a personalised covering letter. If you just send the brochure on its own you run the risk of appearing too impersonal, and the customer may think you are too busy to handle requests for modest amounts of work.

A brochure also helps when you are looking for business writing work, or when you are asking someone important if you can interview them. It gives everyone confidence that you are here to stay.

Advertising

Advertising can work in some very specialised cases, but it can also prove to be an expensive failure. If you have the budget, however, it can be a way of:

- making your name and availability known to people who might need you
- and making sure that they have your telephone number in front of them at the moment when they need you.

Is It Worth Marketing Yourself?

Any promotion, whether it is a direct mail campaign or an advertisement, can still be called a success if it only produces one response. For instance, you might spend several hundred pounds on an advertisement which only produces one reply, but that one reply comes from a publisher who wants a book which will earn you several thousand pounds. A direct mail campaign might go to a thousand people and the one who responds may give you enough work to last a year.

Obviously, all promotional campaigns should ideally provide the maximum potential response for the minimum outlay, but every so often it is worth taking a risk and spending a bit more to attract new clients of a higher calibre.

When Should You Market Yourself?

The time to invest in promotional campaigns is when you are at your busiest. But this is when you tend not to do so because you don't have the time and because you feel confident that the work will keep coming in.

No matter how much work you have this week, there is no knowing whether anything will come in next week or the week after. It's no reflection on your abilities if the work regularly dries up – it's merely the nature of your business.

Editors move on and stop using freelancers, or hire staff writers who do all the necessary work, or change the slant of the magazine, or simply have to cut their editorial budgets. New freelancers come along and take some of the work you might have got ... There are a million possible reasons why you will always get quiet periods.

The first problem is that when the quiet periods arrive, free-lancers tend to worry (quite rightly) about their cashflow, and they become cautious about spending money on speculative promotional campaigns.

The second problem is that it always takes time before you see the fruits of your labours. If you decide to do a direct mail campaign today it will take a few days, or weeks, to get the necessary addresses, the printed material and the letters prepared. When you send the letters out there might be a gap of another few weeks, or months, before anyone responds. If they commission you to write an article it could then be a couple more months before it appears and a further month before you are paid. The money may not actually reach you until six months or a year after you sent out your letters or placed your advertisement. If you are talking about book publishing it might be even longer than that.

During a busy time, however, you will have the money to pay for a promotional campaign, and the resulting work should come in before you start to experience a downturn.

TWO MORE GOLDEN RULES OF FREELANCING

1 *Never Panic That You Have Too Much Work!*

Never turn work down because you don't think you will have time to do it – there is always time. Only turn it down because it isn't financially viable or because you don't want to do it. If you turn an editor down once they may never come back to you again.

There have been times when I have been working on five books simultaneously, and doing articles and business writing on the side, and I have felt strongly tempted to panic and start trying to get out of some of the projects. Experience has taught me, however, that out of five major projects, one will be cancelled, two will be delayed, and one of the remaining two will prove to be easier than you expected.

Having said that, you should always let your customers know the situation. Explain that you have other things on (they will appreciate the fact that you are in demand) and give them sensible dates by which you can deliver the work. If it has to be rushed through, see if any of your other projects are running ahead of schedule and can be interrupted for a rush job.

It sometimes helps, in the middle of a large project like a book, to take a break for a week or two in order to do something completely different. You can then return to the job, which might have been becoming rather a burden, refreshed and full of new enthusiasm.

2 *Always Be Available*

Someone who rings up to commission work does not want to know about your problems. They do not want to hear you sighing that you are already behind on six other projects and that your dog has died so you are finding it hard to concentrate.

They want to hear that you are keen to work on their project. They want to tick it off their list, confident that it will arrive well before the deadline they have given you.

Most of all, they want a speedy response. They really want to talk to you today, otherwise they may ring someone else. If they can't speak to you personally they want to leave a message on your answering machine and then know that you will ring back as soon as possible – certainly no later than the following day.

5

Getting
the Information

'Don't believe everything you read in the papers.'

It's a cliché, but of course it's true. It's not that journalists and writers deliberately set out to mislead anyone – well, not usually anyway – it's just that they are often expressing their subjective opinions, or the subjective opinions of the people they have interviewed. Pressure of time means that their research is never quite as extensive as it should be, and sometimes they will be misled by interested parties. Something you read in a paper is as likely to be inaccurate or one-sided as something you hear in a classroom, at a dinner party, or on top of a bus.

At some stage a writer has to decide that they know enough about a subject to write usefully on it. The more quickly they can reach that stage the more cost-effective it will be. If you are being paid £200 for an article, you can't spend a month researching it – it's as simple as that.

This does not mean you can get away without thorough research (because something which is under-researched won't sell). It just means that you need to use the most efficient methods of gathering information.

At the beginning of your career you will have to do more research on everything you write about because you are still relatively inexperienced and it will therefore be harder to persuade editors to use you.

WHERE DO YOU START?

When you have been asked to write an article on a subject you know nothing about, it can be difficult to know where to start. The skill lies in knowing who to talk to about what, and in judging which bits of information are likely to be true and/or useful to your readers.

Often you will be writing for an audience which already knows a considerable amount about the subject. They will therefore expect you to be able to teach them something they didn't know before. As you're unlikely to have this sort of expert knowledge already, you need to search out your material.

When you are starting from scratch like this, you can set off in almost any direction, because by asking the right questions you will eventually be guided to the most fruitful areas for enquiry. It means going up a lot of blind alleys along the way, but that all adds to your experience.

As time goes on, you will start to find your way to the sources of information more quickly — one telephone call instead of six, or a trip to the filing cabinet rather than out in the car to interview someone.

Following the Editor's Brief

Briefs from editors can vary. Sometimes they might say 'go and find out about this subject', or 'go and interview this person', in which case your path is fairly straightforward. You simply have to ask questions and keep asking them until you feel you have sufficient grasp of the subject to write about it helpfully.

At other times, however, the editor will have a preconceived idea of what stance the article should take, and you will be asked to find evidence to support that argument. Or you may have come to a conclusion yourself about a subject, but need to give your words weight by finding other people willing to endorse them. This can be harder.

Sometimes an editor might be trying to manufacture a controversy where there isn't one, or where everyone involved is trying very hard to avoid conflict. The people you contact for a story like this will consequently not welcome the idea of an article stirring up dissent, and will almost certainly have to be tricked into being indiscreet.

If you need the work badly enough you will have to take it and just keep on ringing people until you find someone who for some reason shares the editor's prejudices and is willing to be quoted as such. However, it would be better if you could persuade the editor that there wasn't really a story there and suggest an alternative angle.

Finding People to Ask

Unless you are writing an article as an acknowledged expert in the subject, you are going to have to quote other people, either by name or by description (e.g. 'a leading nuclear scientist said ...'). So how do you judge the best people to go to?

Start by asking the editor if there is anyone they would particularly like you to talk to. The chances are that they will mention some names of people who have something useful to say. If they don't give you any names, ask if there are any particular organisations they would like you to consult on the subject. While you want to leave the editor feeling confident that you know what you are doing, you also want to have as many names as possible to start you off.

If the editor is unable or unwilling to give you any leads, you'll need to use your memory and imagination. Start off by recalling anything else you may have read on the subject. Check your clippings library and any recent publications for useful names − not just the author of the book or article but the experts they quote. Your local reference library should provide further names. Then track them down any way you can − through directory enquiries, professional directories, their place of work, or someone else who might know them.

Talking to Companies

If you are given company or organisation names, but not individuals, the in-house public relations or press offices will be the best places to start. In some cases they will refer you to their public relations consultancies. The disadvantage of this is that public relations consultants don't usually know very much themselves. The advantage, however, is that they need to impress their clients with as much press coverage as possible. So, as long as you are writing constructively about their business and are not out to expose them in some way, the PR consultant will be a good ally.

Whoever it is you are put on to, explain what you need, and ask them firstly if they can help you with some information, or secondly if they know of anyone in their organisation who would have opinions on the subject. Everyone you contact should be asked if they know of anyone else you should be talking to. They will nearly always come up with one or two names.

It always helps if you can tell them that you are writing the article for a specific publication. If they don't know you they will be unwilling to give any information without knowing where it's going to end up. If you haven't got a specific editor lined up to buy the piece, explain that you are a freelance, and tell them which magazine you are hoping to place the article in.

INTERVIEWING TECHNIQUES

When you are starting out it's a good idea to interview as many people as possible in person. That way you get more of their time and attention. You also get a better idea of the setting in which they operate, and consequently a clearer idea of why they might be saying what they are saying.

Many people, when first approached by a writer, start by giving the impression that they don't really have anything worth saying. Once they actually start talking, however, they get carried away by their own train of thought, and it can then be hard to stop them. The ones who tell you they could write a book on the subject often turn out to have the least to say.

Put People at Their Ease

Interviewees are often much more nervous than you. That means they may be reticent and shy, or they may be gushing and indiscreet. To get the most from them you have to put them at their ease and make them like you.

Prepare Your Questions in Advance

Have a clear idea of what you are going to ask them. It is wise to write down at least three or four main subject areas that you want to cover. That doesn't mean that you can't stray into new territory, but it gives you something to ask them at the beginning, to set them off in the right direction.

If supplementary questions occur to you while they are talking, jot them down to ask later. Otherwise you will have forgotten them by the time the next opportunity for a question arises, or you will be concentrating so hard on remembering your next question that you won't be able to listen to what they are saying.

If you are feeling nervous about meeting or talking to the interviewee, prepare a lot of questions in advance, in case your mind becomes clouded by stage fright and you need a prompt to refer to.

Most face-to-face interviews last about an hour, so you need enough questions to fill that amount of time if you are hoping to get a decent-length article out of it.

Don't Ask Closed Questions

Never ask closed questions, which can be answered with a simple 'yes' or 'no', otherwise you will run out of conversation very quickly, and will not come away with any useful material. Here are some examples.

Closed question: 'Do you enjoy sport?'
Open question: 'Which sports do you enjoy most?'
Follow-up question: 'Why is that?'

Remember that Interviews are Conversations

An interview is just a formalised conversation. You need to stimulate the interviewee, through questions and suggestions which they can accept or reject, into giving you an insight into their subject.

A good way to start, therefore, is to tell them what you think the theme of the article is going to be, and to ask them if they think that is the best approach. Whether they think it is or not, you can follow up with further questions, which should elicit the material you need.

Don't be Frightened of Silence

Don't be afraid to leave silences after they finish speaking, firstly because it gives the impression that you are thinking about what they have said, and secondly because they may well feel the need to cover the silence by blurting out something more interesting than they intended.

Always Keep a Record

It is vital that you keep a record of everything that is said during an interview, particularly if it is a subject with which you are not completely familiar. You may well be able to understand what they are saying at the time, but if you don't get round to writing the piece until a couple of days later you may have a great deal of difficulty remembering. Also if you're accused of misquoting the person at some later date, you may need to produce tangible evidence.

A tape-recorder is the most reliable method. If your attention wanders, and you find that you have not been listening to what the interviewee has been saying, at least you know you have the words on record and you can refer back to them later.

A tape-recorder can also make your job a lot easier, particularly if you are writing a whole article from one person's words. If you have a clear idea of the article's final form at the beginning, and you structure your questions accordingly, you can virtually get them to talk their way through it. All you have to do then is transcribe the tape on to your word-processor, and edit the words into shape.

If you are interviewing someone face to face, it's often a good idea to use a notebook as well as a tape-recorder. This helps to relax the interviewee by regularly breaking eye contact when they are talking. If you are just using a tape-recorder you can end up staring at them in a rather unnerving manner.

Always Confess your Ignorance

If they say something you don't understand, or use a term which you are unfamiliar with, be quick to ask them what they mean. If you pretend to understand, in the hope of finding out later, you may have begun to lose the thread of what is being said. You will also have given them a false impression of the extent of your knowledge. If you don't stop and ask for an explanation they may use more and more jargon, and start to talk on more and more complex levels, until you get completely lost.

As you gain experience you will become more knowledgeable about certain subjects, or will at least learn enough about them to carry on sensible conversations with the real experts.

Never be Afraid to Ask Rude Questions

Many of us are reluctant to ask people direct questions, especially about really interesting things. One of the perks of being a writer, however, is that you can be nosey. You can ask people how they make their living, how much money they make, what their private lives are like and all sorts of other things. If they get upset you can apologise and blame your professional habits.

Most people, when asked a straight question, will not only give a straight answer, they will pour out a great deal more than you ever expected. It is almost as if they are relieved to unburden themselves to someone who actually seems interested.

Naturally there are some people who will refuse to answer, but they usually do so with good humour. And in many cases they only refuse to answer because they haven't got anything interesting to say.

Never Argue

Never get into a personal argument, no matter how strongly you disagree with the interviewee. You are there to find out their opinions, not to win them over to yours. If you think there are serious faults in what they say, tell them you have heard something different from another source, and then listen to how they argue their case. If you make it a personal argument they will stop being completely open with you.

Even if you still disagree with what they say when you come to write the piece, it doesn't matter, because you are going to put it in quotes. Readers who want to dispute it will then be taking issue with the interviewee, not with you. Your job is to lay out the interviewee's arguments as fully as possible, for other people to judge whether they are right or wrong, foolish or wise.

Use the Phone to its Best Advantage

If you are doing the interview over the phone and the interviewee asks how long it is likely to take, say 'just a few minutes'. If they prove to have nothing useful to say you can then escape quickly. If they prove to have a great deal to say they will soon get into their stride and forget the time.

If they seem to be fruitful sources of information, but they don't have time to speak to you when you ring, ask when it would be convenient to ring them back – and make sure you do. This can have a number of advantages:

- It flatters them by showing that you genuinely value their opinion.
- It gives them time to think about the subject and to come up with more thoughtful answers.
- It gives you time to talk to other people and increase your own knowledge of the subject.

For a full-length article you may need to talk to six or seven experts. You might have a list of names and numbers, all of which you ring in succession, only to find that none of them are in, or they are busy, or you can't get through. You leave lots of messages and then ... nothing happens. So you panic and ring six more people, achieve only a modicum of success, and begin to despair of ever getting enough material for a whole article.

Try to be patient, because suddenly you will find that they are all calling you back at the end of the day, or the following morning, and you are being given enough material to write a book. Talk to all of them, even when you think you have enough material for the article, and try to include as many as possible in the final piece. Try their ideas out on one another, e.g. 'So and so told me such and such. Would you agree?' That way you can check that you aren't going to print anything which is too wide of the mark.

Use Interviews to Build Up Your Contacts

If you are planning to write frequently about a particular subject, then it pays to build up a relationship with good information sources. You might, for instance, send them photocopies of the article when it is published with a note thanking them for their help.

Contacts you make through interviews can also lead to public relations and corporate writing work (see Chapter 13). One of the best ways to get work is through personal recommendation. Someone you have met, or talked to on the phone, may well think of using you when they have a job of their own. So it is worth getting into casual conversation, explaining that you are freelance, and that you do a lot of work in their particular field.

If they show the slightest interest, offer to send them details. If you have nothing printed, just write them a letter so that they will have your name and number on file should they ever need to use your services. (This is where business cards are essential, and some sort of leaflet, brochure or curriculum vitae would be helpful.)

Store your Information

Always keep people's names, titles, telephone numbers and addresses on file. By building a network of contacts, you start to cut down on the time and effort required on future jobs. And that's when you can start making money.

If you know which areas you are going to specialise in, it's also worth opening cuttings files (cutting out and keeping anything relevant that you come across in the media). You have to be selective, otherwise you could end up spending more time filing than writing. In some cases, however, simply compiling information may provide an income, since you can then create reference works, or lists of contacts to go at the end of practical advice articles.

You might also be able to see new angles on stories by looking back through the cuttings and recognising trends and developments. You might find, for instance, that one of the sources you have quoted in the past is now saying the exact opposite to what he said a year ago. You could then find out why his views have changed, and build that into a story.

WRITING UP INTERVIEWS

Attributed Quotes

It is always safer to put statements into quotation marks if you are not entirely sure that you agree with them. If you state them as facts, you lay yourself open to being proved wrong. If, on the other hand, you say, 'Many people in the industry believe such and such', and go on to quote what someone said to you in order to illustrate the point, then you have transferred any culpability on to them.

For instance, unless you have a thorough knowledge of the industry, you're probably not qualified to assert that 'the widget industry is in decline and is unlikely to recover'. It would be much better to use an attributed quote: *'The widget industry is in decline,' says John Smith, Chairman of Widgets International, 'and is unlikely to recover.'*

To get this sort of quote you simply need to have asked John Smith a question such as, 'What state is the widget industry in?'

Once you have Mr Smith's opinion you can then go to one of his competitors and say, 'John Smith says . . .' His rival may then agree or disagree, which gives you another quote and builds either a case or a controversy, depending on the answer.

Comments Off the Record

If someone tells you that they are talking 'off the record', then you should respect their request, otherwise you will never be able to go back to them for more information. Only if they trust you not to embarrass them will they tell you the really juicy bits of scandal and gossip.

Either you can use what they say without attributing it to them, or you can ask someone else, who isn't afraid to be quoted, if they agree with whatever it is they've said, and then quote the latter person.

Once they have started talking to you, many people will relax and forget that you are intending to write an article. They will answer your questions just as they would if they met you at a dinner party. Suddenly, as you near the end of the conversation (probably when you ask them how they spell their name, or what their title is), the awful truth will dawn on them that their own words may be quoted in the pages of a newspaper. They begin to wonder if what they've said might upset their bosses, their friends or their customers, and they panic.

This is when they sometimes ask to see a copy of the article before it is published so that they can 'check the facts'. While it might make sense to do this if you are hoping to build any sort of future relationship with the interviewee, it is not always practical.

If you have talked to six or seven people for a 1,000-word article, for example, you won't have time to send copies to all of them and then incorporate all their corrections. (Nobody can resist changing something when they see it in black and white.)

There will be cases, however, where you genuinely need to check that you are on the right lines, or where you have a vested interest in building a relationship of mutual trust, or where the person is just too important for you to refuse.

In such cases, you can ring them when you have written the piece, and read their quotes back to them. Or, if there is time, you can send them copies of the article.

On the whole, however, it's probably easier not to name these people as sources, and look for other people who don't mind putting their names to controversial statements in print.

Anyone who earns a living from supplying investigative news stories to the national media will probably be rocking with laughter at this squeamishness, believing that the only things worth printing are the things people don't want you to print. However this is a specialised area of journalism, usually undertaken by newspaper staffers. Freelancers who go in for investigative and exposé reporting need to have a killer instinct and an unlimited source of new contacts. If the stories they uncover are big enough they can make a lot of money. If they aren't, they simply make a lot of enemies.

If you plan to get involved in this sort of writing you should be aware of the provisions of the libel laws in your country (see p. 211).

USING WRITTEN MATERIAL

It is always a great relief to find that someone has already written a book or article on precisely the subject you have to cover, so that all you have to do is read up on it. But where do you draw the line between learning from the text and copying it?

You can use the very best bits as quotes, 'as Professor Humpkin says in his book on the Peruvian Indians ...'. However, bear in mind that if you quote from a published source at any length the publisher may require payment. (For more on copyright law and permission fees, see p. 210).

For the most part, you should study the book or article and supplement it with as many other sources as possible. Just as a university student will study a textbook and then write a thesis on the subject it covers, you can study your sources, perhaps making bullet point notes which will not plagiarise the actual words of the original, and then communicate the content to your readers.

Once you feel you have understood the subject, you can write about it in your own words, taking your own slant, and perhaps mixing and matching the theories and findings of two or more experts.

Again we come back to what you, as a writer, are selling, which is your understanding of a subject and your ability to communicate it. If you slavishly copy out someone else's work, you will not only be putting yourself in the wrong legally, you will also be doing a very poor job, because it will mean that you haven't fully understood the subject.

6

Local Papers

Local papers do not have much money, but they do provide an excellent starting point for getting your work published. If you are at the beginning of your career, and you need to gain experience, the local papers in your area could provide a useful outlet.

HOW DO YOU APPROACH THEM?

Contact the editors and ask if there are any areas they have difficulty in getting material on. They may tell you that everything is covered by their staff writers, but it could be that someone has just left, or they are understaffed and unable to get to every event they should cover.

At the same time as contacting the editors, you should research and write a story. This will demonstrate your writing skills and you can also try to sell it to them.

WHAT SORT OF STORIES DO THEY WANT?

Stories About Local People

Local papers need stories about people who live within their area and who are doing something interesting. The papers will seek out these people themselves when they can, but they can't be everywhere or meet everyone. Start by thinking of all the people you know or have heard of, and ask yourself which ones you would be interested in finding out more about. If no one comes to mind, ask other people about interesting characters they know, or people who are doing interesting things.

If the stories also tell the readers about a service they can use, or a place they can visit, so much the better.

It will help to sell your story if you can provide a photograph as well — probably black and white (although more and more papers are starting to use colour).

While ferreting out these unusual stories you may also come up with ideas for the national press and other media. You might, for instance, interview someone who keeps bees and sells the honey to local shops. That story could be of interest to a local editor, but while talking to this person you might discover that beekeeping is a lucrative hobby which anyone can indulge in, if they approach it the right way. You can then find a few more beekeepers to talk to in other parts of the country, which could give you the basis of a 'how to keep bees' article, or even a book idea.

Talking to these beekeepers might also produce a number of anecdotes about what happens when the bees swarm in other people's gardens and houses, which would make a humorous piece for a magazine or newspaper.

Stories About Local Issues

There may also be a local issue which you know about and which would be of burning interest to other people, whether it is the problem of litter in your high street or plans to build a housing estate in a beautiful bit of countryside. The secret is to get as many other people to give you quotes on the subject as possible. If you write down all your own opinions you will merely get printed in the letters column, but if you go round soliciting quotes from other locals who will be affected by the issue, you can start to build a proper story.

SYNDICATION

Syndication is big business in America, where, until very recently, there were no national papers. Because they are spread across the country to serve the needs of separate readerships, there is little or no overlap, so papers in all the different cities and states can publish the same material – if it is relevant – at the same time.

Some of the best-known columnists can therefore end up making a great deal of money because they can sell one article to as many as 200 different outlets. However, the article has to be as relevant to readers in New Orleans as it is to readers in New York or San Francisco.

The same principles can apply in other countries, but on a far smaller scale. For example, because Britain is so well served by its national press, there is only a handful of local daily papers. Some of these local papers, like the London *Evening Standard*, are very powerful publications. The rest of the local press consists of weekly papers which have virtually no budget with which to pay freelancers and very little interest in anything which comes from outside their specific areas.

None of the editors will mind you selling your articles to other papers, as long as there is no overlap of readership. It's wise, however, when you win a new customer, to let all your existing outlets know about it, in case there is some conflict of interest which you know nothing about. In some cases, for instance, several papers in different areas may be owned by the same company.

Initially you should contact every editor separately and simply sell them the idea or article. No contracts or even letters of acceptance will normally be exchanged (few editors have time for such formalities), unless you are entering into a regular relationship, agreeing to supply something every week or month.

If an editor asks you to sign a contract which would give them sole rights to the article, and would stop you selling it to anyone else, decline to sign it. However, this situation is very unlikely to occur. As long as you ensure that the article does not appear in directly competing media everyone will be happy.

You Need an Idea with Legs

To make syndication worthwhile, you need to be able to supply regular columns, not one-off articles. The amount of time and money you would have to invest in sending individual articles round to local editors would not justify the occasional small fees you would be paid. If, however, you can persuade an editor to take a column every week, you then have a regular flow of income, and a readymade product which you can offer to other, non-competing, publications.

The sort of subjects which are most useful to local newspaper editors are practical advice pieces. If you can produce a gardening column that tells people what they should be doing every week of the year, or a DIY column that covers a different topic each week, or a personal financial advice column, then your words will be relevant to all readers wherever they live.

Preparing Your Proposal

Prepare a proposal to send to the editors which explains what you want to do for them. Include a list of the subjects you would like to cover in the first six months or year of your series. Here are two examples.

1 WHAT'S HAPPENING DOWN ON THE FARM
This series of articles will explain, month by month, what is happening in fields and barns all over the countryside, so that people passing by on the roads and walking in the countryside can gain an understanding of what they see.
Subjects to be covered would include:

- The Burning of Stubble: Why do farmers do this? Is it dangerous to the local wildlife? Are there any alternatives?
- Planting Time: Which crops are being planted this month?
- Protecting the Crops: How can the public help farmers protect their crops from damage?
- Lambing Time: What happens at lambing time?

2 LOOKING AFTER YOUR FINANCES

This series of articles will look, week by week, at different aspects of personal finance.

Subjects to be covered would include:

- Choosing a personal pension.
- Making sure you can afford your mortgage.
- Dealing with debt.
- Choosing a high street bank to suit your needs.
- The advantages of building societies versus banks for personal savings.
- Reducing the burden of inheritance tax on your children.

These examples give a rough idea of how to structure your ideas. You would need to use your personal knowledge of the subject to make them more extensive, and to convince the editors that you would be able to provide enough material for each article.

The next step is to write one sample article (around 500 words would probably be enough) to show the sort of style you have in mind.

Once you have created this package you can send it off to as many local papers as you can find. There are a number of reference books available (see Useful Addresses) which list publications with addresses, the names of their editors, their circulation figures and other information to help you judge their relative importance.

Bear in mind that some of them will have overlapping readerships, so check where they are on the map first, and then send your ideas to the ones with the biggest circulations, or the most frequent publishing schedules. A paper which publishes daily, for instance, is going to need more editorial than one which only comes out once a week. Likewise, one which has 20,000 readers will have more money to spend on editorial than one with 2,000, and so on.

Send your package off with a covering letter explaining why you think the articles will be of interest to their readers, and enclose a stamped addressed envelope to make it easy for them to respond. You need to know which papers are not interested in the suggestion so that you can look for others to cover the same area.

None of these papers will pay a great deal for your work, but if you can write for enough of them, they will be a useful supplement to your income. In the long term they could provide a stepping stone to more profitable activities.

7

National Papers

Many writers aspire to writing in the national papers, believing that it will give them some sort of credibility. They are right – although the amount of credibility they gain will depend on the title concerned.

Appearing regularly in one of the country's major newspapers is an excellent springboard for anything else you might want to do. It can help you get television work, book publishing contracts and other journalism and business writing work, assuming that your specialities lead you in one of those directions.

It has become easier to get published in the national press since the number of titles increased so dramatically in the 1980s. All these papers are competing for readers and need a constant supply of new and interesting ideas for editorial.

The difficulty is that they have a great many staff writers, journalists and reporters who need to be kept permanently occupied. They also have access to established – or even famous – experts on almost any topic they are likely to cover. However, if they really like or need freelance ideas or stories, they will pay generously for them.

WHAT SORT OF MATERIAL DO THEY WANT?

Unusual Stories

Most national papers will be willing to pay for a story that is so original they haven't thought it up for themselves.

It is no good, for instance, suggesting an interview with the Prime Minister or President because they have staff who can do this for them already, unless you have special access which might be denied to any other reporter.

If, however, you have just returned from a one-man expedition to the South Pole, or have completed some research into why people get married which has revealed some startling facts about love, lust and the human condition, then you have an advantage over anyone working for them full-time.

Specialist Columns

The other line of approach is to offer specialist knowledge of one particular subject. Ideally you will then be adopted by a paper as their technology correspondent, gardening correspondent, marketing correspondent, cookery correspondent or whatever your subject might be. Being a regular correspondent will then be a great help in selling your services to other buyers.

HOW DO YOU APPROACH THEM?

As with other media, the only way to get into the nationals is to approach them regularly and methodically with ideas and articles you have already written.

Research Your Market

The danger is that you will inundate them with unsuitable work which they will reject, and they may begin to regard you as a nuisance rather than a possible resource. So, before you send something in, make sure:

1   That it is going to the right person.

2   That you truly believe it is the sort of thing they are likely
    to print.

It is no good sending in something which you know, in your
heart of hearts, is inferior, in the hope that they will edit it into
shape. They are offered too much material to have to do that.
(They will edit it, but only if they can see at a glance that it is
highly relevant to their needs.)

Read the paper you want to write for carefully, find out who
edits which parts of it, and then angle your suggestions
carefully to fit in with their needs. It is no good, for instance,
sending stories about the sex lives of pop stars to the quality
papers; and it is equally pointless to send a piece on the merits
of modern dance versus classical ballet to the tabloids.

Keep It Concise

If you are sending a suggestion – and it is nearly always better
to do this first – make sure you can explain the idea in one
short paragraph, and then say something about why you think
it would be of interest to their readers.

If you are sending a complete article, keep it down to
between 500 and 1,000 words and make sure that the subject is
obvious from the title and the opening words.

INVESTIGATIVE STORIES

If you have managed to uncover something which would either
be impossible for another reporter to follow up in time, or
would be extremely expensive for editors to put their own
people on to, then you have a commodity for which you should
be able to get a premium price.

There are some freelancers who do nothing but investigative
reporting – usually writers who have spent some years working
on national papers full-time and therefore know how to go
about digging out a story which others would prefer to keep
hidden.

If the story appeals to editors in America and Europe as well as your own country, it may earn you enough money to live on for a year. That sounds good, but bear in mind that it may have taken you a year to uncover the story, and it might be a great deal longer before you come across another one as good.

This is a hard line of business to be in. It requires a great deal of luck, and a lot of time spent in the right circles listening to gossip and rumour and then searching out the facts to back up your suspicions.

Occasionally you may come across juicy stories in the pursuit of some other project, like a biography. You then have a double incentive to get into the nationals, since any coverage of the story will help you sell your book, as well as bring you the fee from the paper.

THE FRUSTRATIONS OF DEALING WITH THE NATIONALS

They May Not Use the Article

Editors often agree to buy articles and then don't use them, simply because they don't have the space. If they have commissioned them from you they are obliged to pay a fee, although it may be reduced if they haven't used the piece. If you have sent it in on spec and they say they will use it, but don't, they still have a moral obligation to pay you for it (since you haven't been able to sell it elsewhere while they were planning to run it). Whether or not they honour this obligation will depend on your relationship with the editor concerned. Provided you deal with them firmly and politely, they will probably pay at least part of the fee.

They May Edit It Down to Nothing

When they do buy your work they often edit it down to virtually nothing in order to fit it in. Unless you have agreed the price at the beginning you may then get paid a much smaller 'per word' fee. If you do agree a price when they first accept the piece, I'd advise you to have something in writing, even if it is only a letter from you confirming the deal and enclosing an invoice.

Unlike local papers, the nationals have plenty of money, and in most cases they would rather honour their obligations, provided they think you are being fair with them. You should aim to build such friendly relations with the editors concerned that misunderstandings are kept to a minimum and can be sorted out in a few minutes over the phone.

They May Change Your Meaning

They are quite capable of editing your words so heavily that the article ends up saying something completely different to what you actually meant. If this means that they are printing things under your name which you disagree with, it may annoy you a great deal. In such a case it's sometimes worth writing a letter to the editor to register your displeasure – preferably without endangering the relationship for the future. Since newspapers are such ephemeral things, however, you would probably be wiser to forget it, because everyone else will.

One advantage is that if they do change your article completely, you should then be able to take the original copy and sell it to someone else, since it bears no relation to the piece they have published. If you have a good enough relationship with the editor concerned, you could tell them that you are doing this. Provided you are not selling to a direct rival, they are unlikely to complain. In most cases, as long as there are no longer any direct similarities between the pieces, you are free to submit it to whoever else you choose.

8

Writing for Magazines

An enormous number of new magazines have been launched in every market sector in the last twenty years. Not all of them have survived, but there have been enough success stories to create a permanent pool of thousands of potential customers for a freelance writer. Their needs vary enormously, just as their readerships do, but they have one thing in common – they all need to find material which will interest their readers and keep them turning the pages.

SPECIALIST AND TRADE MAGAZINES

Most magazines make most of their money by selling advertising space. The most popular ones are also able to charge readers a cover price. It is still the advertising, however, which provides the greatest potential profit. As a result some magazines are given away to readers in order to obtain the necessary circulation figures to justify their advertising rates.

To ensure that the people who receive the magazines read at least some of the contents, the editors try to tailor the material as tightly as possible to their specific interests. If you are a professional exhibition organiser there are magazines aimed directly at you; likewise if you run a fast food outlet or a hotel. For every profession, hobby, sport or special interest, there are magazines competing for the attention of the practitioners.

In order to find topics which editors will buy, you have to think about the needs of their readers. The more specialised the subject, the harder the editor is going to find it to uncover new and original things to write about, and the more opportunities there will be for freelancers. However, it will also be harder for the freelance writer to find new angles which are sufficiently important and interesting.

The answer often lies in lateral thinking (finding topics which require expertise from another area, and then applying that expertise to the specialised sectors). For instance, if you have managed to build up a fund of information on pensions, you could adapt the information so that it was of interest to the fish and chip shop owner as well as the keen golfer, the senior manager of a multinational corporation and the ironmonger.

The same would apply if you knew a lot about health in the workplace, training staff or buying office furniture. Most subjects will be of interest to more than one group of people if angled in the right way. An article about how to set up exhibition stands at the lowest possible cost will be of interest to anyone in any industry who ever has to attend an exhibition. It could therefore be sold to a wide variety of publications with virtually no adaptation and little fear that the readerships would overlap.

WOMEN'S MAGAZINES

Women's magazines have always been a good source of income for freelancers. Although many of them have a large number of in-house staff writers, they still need to buy in articles on topical subjects.

There is, of course, an enormous difference in style between magazines aimed at different age groups and income brackets but there are still subjects which can be adapted to fit their various needs.

The readers are very similar to those of the national press, but they obviously spend more time on a magazine. So a 1,000-word article, which is long for a newspaper, is rather short for a magazine. Some magazines will publish 4,000 or 5,000 words on particularly interesting subjects. Since words are usually bought by the thousand, this makes magazine commissions far more profitable for the freelance writer.

As well as one-off, lengthy articles, magazines also need regular features. If they prove popular, these regular features can end up being major selling points for the magazine. They are usually on certain standard subjects and are not too demanding in terms of time, leaving the writers free to adapt and expand their knowledge base in order to sell material to several outlets in different forms.

Suppose, for instance, you write a regular monthly column on psychology for a women's magazine. The task would probably only take a few hours of your time if it is a subject you are continuously studying for other professional reasons. However the fee you receive for those few hours might represent a few days' income, and the exposure the magazine gives you could help you gain access to more interesting material for other magazine columns and for books or lectures or whatever else you do.

The same principle applies to virtually any generally popular subject. A writer who has access to material about cookery, for instance, could adapt it to suit any number of different magazines. You could do the same with subjects like love, marriage and child-rearing, although many women's magazines have worked hard in recent years to get away from this image of their readers. They therefore need a steady stream of articles on careers and the world of work to balance the traditional material on home and children.

MEN'S MAGAZINES

These also fall into a number of categories. There are soft porn magazines which also carry general interest articles, and there are hobby magazines covering everything from soldiering to four-wheel-drive vehicles.

Although some glossy men's 'lifestyle' magazines have been launched in recent years, this is still a very small market for freelancers, especially since much of their material comes from big-name writers. However, like all magazines, they are always in need of good stories.

SPECIAL FEATURES

Because trade magazines are so dependent on advertising, they frequently run special features. This means that they dedicate a number of pages to a specific topic, and sell advertising on the strength of it.

A national paper, for instance, might run special features on anything from a particular city or region to power stations or the packaging industry. A marketing magazine might run special features on conference organisation, corporate hospitality, exhibitions or sales promotion. They then need to find two, three or even more articles to justify calling it a special feature, and that is when they become desperate for freelance help.

These special features usually come round at least once, and sometimes twice, a year. The staff writers very quickly run out of enthusiasm for writing about the same old subjects, so a freelancer who can think up new ideas on old subjects, or provide interesting material to fit their ideas, is going to be very popular indeed.

Most publications produce lists of forthcoming special features at the beginning of each year. These are available from their advertising departments, and are also collated by some enterprising firms into lists which are circulated regularly to interested parties (see the 'Directories' section under Useful Addresses).

If you have a great deal of material on a subject – say the motor industry – it would be worth finding out when magazines are doing special features on cars, and then sending them a list of suggested angles you could cover for them. You will find many of them very grateful indeed.

HOW DO YOU APPROACH MAGAZINE EDITORS?

Many magazines never appear on the news stands. So you will need to consult one of the reference books which lists them all (see the 'Directories' and 'Media Guides' sections under Useful Addresses).

Even with a list of titles, addresses and names, it is still hard to tell which magazines will use material from freelancers and which ones will be able to pay reasonable rates. Sometimes a title which sounds very esoteric is actually owned by a large newspaper or publishing corporation and has the resources to pay well for contributions; while a title which sounds very grand may be little more than a newsletter produced in somebody's spare bedroom.

The first step is to write to all the titles which look as if they might be potential buyers, with an outline of your idea or a copy of the article you hope to sell. If you are sending an idea, you should also include a sample of your work (published if possible, since that will give them more confidence in your professional status), and a brief outline of your professional background, in so far as it is relevant to the article.

They will not necessarily reply to a letter, so if your mailing hasn't produced a sufficient number of responses after a few weeks, you will need to follow it up with telephone calls.

Keep a careful note of the editors' answers, so that you don't waste time later approaching people who never use freelance articles or who can't pay for them.

Magazine editors are not the most organised people in the world, and the fact that they haven't answered your letter doesn't necessarily mean that they aren't interested. It is more likely to mean that it has simply disappeared under mounds of other material on their desks.

Magazines will amost certainly form part of your portfolio of customers, because they are too big a potential market for you to ignore.

9

Selling Fiction

Can you think of any more perfect way of earning a living than spending all your time inventing your own worlds, populating them with characters and weaving stories about them? If you write fiction you can take total control of your work, and move it in any direction you want. It is certainly a wonderful thing to be able to do — but how on earth do you make a living at it?

THE FACTS

This is the most competitive area of writing, and the one where it is hardest to make a sale. So, before you start your first novel, look the facts fairly and squarely in the face:

- Only a tiny percentage of the novels which are started ever get finished.
- Publishers will be able to tell at a glance whether they want to read the first page.
- By the end of the first page they will know if they want to read the next couple of pages.
- By page three they will almost certainly have given up and sent it back.

- You are going to have to write the whole manuscript, investing enormous amounts of time and energy, before you will know for sure if you are going to be able to sell it. The odds against success will be massive.
- Even if your book gets published you will earn virtually no money, and the book will vanish off bookshop shelves within months.
- Even if you have one novel published, that does not mean you will be able to repeat the achievement for years, or ever.

Against all these factors there is only one thought that will keep you going:

'You will never know unless you try.'

It is always possible that, despite the odds, you are one of the gifted few who will be able to make a living from fiction.

Despite all these harsh facts, many of us still cherish the dream, mainly because successful novelists are amongst the most fêted people in the world. Vast amounts of media time and space are devoted to their lives, their thoughts, their money and their work.

To write a best-seller is like winning the pools – it brings fame, wealth and glory out of all proportion to the work involved. So, just as millions of people do the pools each week, knowing full well that the chances against winning are astronomical, many of us continue to produce fiction.

For most people, fiction writing can never be more than a hobby. If it is a vocation which you are willing to starve for, then you will probably succeed in the end, after a great deal of pain. For most writers, particularly at the beginning of their careers, fiction is not a viable way of earning a living on its own. It can, however, be part of your portfolio of work.

There is no reason why you shouldn't keep trying to write fiction and, with even sporadic success over the years, build up a decent body of work. Fiction may even generate you a little income. And the longer you keep trying, of course, the better the odds that you will one day produce a best-seller.

THINK ABOUT THE PUBLISHER

Just for a moment imagine what it must be like to be a publisher. Every day more unsolicited manuscripts land on your desk – hundreds, perhaps thousands, every year. They are enormous and often hard to store in your small office. It is also impossible for you to find time to read them all.

Publishing a work by an unknown writer means gambling a great deal of money – a little of it going to the author, a lot to the printer, more to the sales people, not to mention warehouse costs, vans for distribution and the rest of the machine needed to get the book to the readers.

Yet hardly anyone reads novels, unless they are by famous names, or are part of some genre, such as romance, science fiction or horror stories, all of which can be aimed at a target group of people who have already shown a liking for that genre.

Now imagine yourself back in the bookshop, looking round the fiction department. Look how many titles there are. How many of them have you read, let along bought? How many do you suppose your best friend, spouse, mother or great-aunt have read? Even if you are a really voracious reader, there are probably no more than twenty or thirty books on the shelves which you have actually paid any money for.

So, assuming the poor publisher finds time to plough through all the manuscripts which are sent in, how do you suppose they will be able to finance and sell your book amongst all this competition? How can you make the publisher's job easier?

Given that they can tell within a few pages whether or not they're interested in your book, why send them the whole manuscript? If you send them a synopsis of the plot, with the first few pages or the first chapter, they will start off by being grateful to you for saving them time.

They will know that you have written the opening pages to the best of your ability. If they are not grabbed by what you have to say here, they certainly won't be by the rest of the manuscript. (The same goes for the reader who, you hope, will one day be picking your book up in the bookshop.)

Make the synopsis as brief as you possibly can, and as tempting. Tell them exactly which sector of the market you think it will appeal to, and why, and then trust their judgement.

Remember to enclose a stamped addressed envelope, so that they won't have to pay to write back to you – it's simple courtesy.

You won't actually be able to sell the book to a publisher until you have written the whole manuscript, but at least this way you can find out whether any publishers are likely to be interested.

DEALING WITH REJECTION

Fiction writing is a very subjective business – look at the conflicting reviews published books receive. One critic might hail a book as a masterpiece while another dismisses the same work as rubbish. There is no way you can make your work appeal to every publisher – although most of them will know whether it is publishable or not in a general sense.

Most publishers also have clear ideas of the sorts of books they want to publish, as well as the numbers of books they can afford to back. So even if your manuscript is perfectly viable for one publisher, you might send it to six others, none of whom feel it fits into their plans, before finding that one.

If publishers don't have reasonably well thought-out plans, and if they publish everything that comes in which seems to have been written to a sufficiently high standard, they will soon be out of business, being unable to sell all the products they are creating.

Rejection is probably worse for would-be novelists than anyone else, partly because the product is so personal, and partly because it takes so much time and effort to create full-length fiction.

Everyone has different ways of dealing with rejection. Some people simply accept that they have not been able to make a sale for any number of reasons, while others feel they are being snubbed by some sort of invisible closed shop or 'old boy network'. Others take a more patronising attitude, pitying the publishers for their shortsightedness in not recognising new talent.

The harsh fact is that no one but you, and the few people closest to you, will care if your work isn't published. All truly remarkable and life-enhancing works are published eventually, and a great deal of dross also finds its way on to the shelves. Arrogant writers stand little chance of succeeding – unless they are real geniuses. Those who understand what readers want, and are able to give it to them, will always find publishers eager to help them with the task and share the rewards.

It may help to bear in mind that just because you are unable to market your fictional creations when you are twenty, it doesn't mean you won't succeed at forty, or sixty. Fiction writing is a skill which flourishes with experience. The more you know and understand about life, the more likely it is that your fictional creations will give readers some insight into themselves and the human condition.

Working as a factual writer is an excellent way to gain the necessary breadth and depth of knowledge while you are waiting to write the material you truly want to write. It also means that you can keep practising the technical skills of writing, and finding out about the way the publishing industry works.

WHERE DO YOU START?

Before you start on a novel, it's best to have the whole thing mapped out, at least in your head, if not on paper. It may change and develop as you go along, but if you don't know how to end it before you start it will almost certainly grind to a halt or, worse still, never stop.

Ask yourself why anyone else should read this book. What will they get from it? Will it touch them? Will it give them an insight into themselves? Will it tell them about a type of person or a part of the world they knew nothing about? Will it excite them? Will it entertain them? Will they care about the characters? Will they be desperate to find out what happens next?

If it won't do any of these things, if you are just writing it 'because it is there' in your head, it is unlikely to succeed, and you must then decide whether you want to write it for your own satisfaction rather than publication.

Next, you must ask yourself why anyone should publish it. How can you convince a publisher that enough people will want to buy your work? How are they going to be able to convince the bookshops to buy large quantities of the book and display it prominently? Does it fit into any particular category of book which is easily marketable?

If you decide that it's worth going ahead, it's very helpful to have an ally during the writing process. For many writers it is almost physically painful to hear other people's opinions of their work. For exactly that reason you should try to get someone else's input. The best person would be an agent, someone who has professional experience, and who you will respect enough to listen to. Unfortunately good agents are in great demand, so it can be quite difficult to find one who is prepared to take you on (for more on finding agents, see Chapter 17).

Assuming you can find an agent, when they first tell you what is wrong with your work you may reject their opinions out of hand, and dismiss them as 'not appreciating' your skills. After you have recovered from the initial hurt, however, you may well find that you can actually improve what you have written with their help. They know what they can sell to publishers.

In the absence of an agent, show your work to any friend or colleague who is willing to give an opinion, and whose views you respect. If you believe that you, and only you, can touch your precious work, you may find it takes longer to get published than if you let other people help you.

WHAT DO YOU WANT TO WRITE?

Literary Novels

It may be that you are a literary genius. Your words may flow with such ease and grace from day one that publishers will be falling over themselves to get you into print, knowing that in the long run you will prove to be a valuable asset.

If this is the case, your talent will be spotted very quickly and you will be looked after with great care by somebody.

Few literary geniuses, however, are able to write commercially successful works, particularly in the early stages of their careers. The potential audience for a piece of literature may be as many as a few thousand, or perhaps even a few hundred thousand, but not all these people are going to buy everything that comes out, especially since they can get much of it from the public libraries for nothing. So a publisher can never hope to sell more than a few thousand copies of a literary novel by an unknown author, and might well sell fewer than a hundred.

Even if you are a genius, it is going to be years before you can earn a decent living from writing the sort of fiction you enjoy. In the long term, of course, you will gain recognition and respect for what you have achieved. Most of us, however, are not patient enough to wait for posterity to reward us for our efforts. We just want to make a living.

Genre Books

The other course of action is to decide on a type of book. The romantic novels published by Mills and Boon are an excellent example, being brilliantly marketed and earning their authors enormous incomes. They are produced to a very set formula, right down to the number of pages and the way the stories are constructed. Around them are many other publishers producing romantic fiction for a similar audience to slightly less rigid formulae.

Many writers, most of whom would never dream of reading a Mills and Boon novel themselves, think they can easily produce manuscripts to this formula. They tell themselves that they can use this sort of writing to give themselves an income which will allow them the freedom to write the sort of books they really want to write. It seldom works!

If you don't believe wholeheartedly in what you are writing, the reader will be able to tell, as will the publisher. You have got to love the books, and live your story without cynicism, even if you are constructing it to a formula. If there is a genre which you genuinely enjoy reading, whether it is horror stories, whodunnits or historical bodice-rippers, you should soak yourself in it. Read everything you can find, and then write one yourself – wholeheartedly.

Short Stories

All the discouraging things that can be said about selling literary novels apply to short stories – only more so. The only advantage is that stories are shorter. Consequently you will spend less time creating something which later proves to be unsaleable, and the finished material is less cumbersome and less expensive to send to potential customers.

The disadvantage is that there are far fewer potential customers. Only a tiny number of book publishers produce anthologies of short stories, and usually they come from established authors whose names will sell the books. In most cases they tend to be highly literary works, created more out of love than any real hope of making a living.

Like novels, writing short stories should be regarded as a pleasure rather than a career. The exception could be genre writing again. Women's magazines, for instance, provide a steady market for writers who are able to master the style. And other markets like men's magazines, science fiction journals and cult titles for Western or horror fans all provide potential outlets. On the whole these are areas for enthusiasts, people who know the requirements of the media they are writing for because they read it themselves.

Poetry

The same problems, magnified yet again, apply to the would-be poet. There are hardly any publishing outlets for new poetry because the potential readership is so small, and so unwilling to pay for the privilege of reading poems.

There are specialist magazines, and there are general literary magazines which carry the occasional poem. As a method of making money it is about as good as joining a nunnery! Do it because you have to, or because you love to, but expect to make a living elsewhere.

The one advantage poets have over fiction writers is that their work can be read aloud, either at live readings or on radio and television. As the broadcasting media continue to grow and multiply, most would-be poets would do better concentrating their efforts on getting on to the air before getting into print (although it is hard to convince producers of your merit if you are entirely unpublished). Any poet who has been published in any form – even through his or her own publishing efforts (see Chapter 19) – will have something they can sell to programme-makers.

A few poets strike it lucky and manage to put their words to music, their own or someone else's. If the songs are released they can become licences to print money.

Children's Books

This is another area, like blockbuster airport novels and Mills and Boon romances, which everyone thinks they can succeed in, especially anyone who has children and sees how short and simple many children's books are. As a result, the competition is ferocious, both to attract the attention of publishers and to sell the resulting books off the shelves.

In some cases illustrations are a vital part of the package, and so a writer who can also draw, or who can work in partnership with an illustrator, stands a better chance of attracting the attention of a publisher.

However, if you are not doing the pictures yourself, it's unwise to pay for anyone else to illustrate your story for you. If you are working with a partner, and you both know your work is being done on spec until you can find a publisher, that is fine. But money spent by a writer on illustrations will probably be wasted, since most children's publishers have very definite ideas about what sort of illustrations they want.

Writing children's books is by no means as simple as it looks. Just as some adults have the knack of talking to children as equals, some writers are able to do the same in print, while others come across as patronising or boring. I suspect it is a skill you are born with and that if it doesn't come naturally there isn't much you can do to cultivate it.

Most children's books sell in relatively small numbers. But every so often an idea will take on a life of its own, usually because the characters in the stories are particularly appealing, and the books are adapted for television and go on to become runaway merchandising successes. From Noddy to Paddington Bear, Spot the Dog to the Teenage Mutant Ninja Turtles, there are many examples of characters which have made fortunes for their creators. On the whole, though, children's writers do the work for the love if it and are grateful for the modest incomes they derive.

SO HOW DO YOU MAKE MONEY FROM FICTION?

Once a publisher has decided to publish your book they will usually send you a letter offering terms. These will include a royalty percentage, some of which may be paid in advance. (For more on this, see p.200.) But in fiction the money doesn't usually come from publication of the initial book or story. The money comes from selling on the product you have created.

You may not make much money from the initial sale, but you have been given the stamp of credibility by, ideally, a respected third party in the form of a publisher. Suddenly you can show potential buyers of subsidiary rights a published book, and that is a great deal more impressive than a typed synopsis.

There are possibilities of selling foreign and translation rights; serialisation in newspapers and magazines, both at home and abroad; and film, radio, television and tape rights. All these extras can follow on from a work of fiction which catches the public's imagination. The publisher will usually handle these sorts of sales for you (see p.135).

So, if you want to make money from fiction you need to create a story or a character which can be marketed as a product. However fine the writing may be, if people can't quickly grasp what the story is about, and be attracted to the characters, then it is going to be harder to persuade publishers, film-makers or book-buyers to invest in your work.

This may all sound like catering for philistines, and it certainly does lead to a lot of pre-packaged, low-brow entertainment. However, that is what many people want to read and watch. And some of the best writing in the world also becomes popular because it fits these criteria.

The Jeeves and Wooster characters in P.G. Wodehouse's novels, for instance, or Peter Pan, or Winnie-the-Pooh have been just as successful in catching the imagination of a broad public as James Bond and Superman. From Hercule Poirot to Tarzan, Count Dracula to Doctor Frankenstein, Miss Marple to My Little Pony, the characters are all instantly recognisable and therefore easily merchandised.

Even if a work of fiction appears to be easy to understand, it can still have depths of meaning which will satisfy readers at a variety of intellectual levels. C.S. Lewis's tales of Narnia or George Orwell's *Animal Farm* can be read at any number of different levels, but they are highly marketable because their major themes are easy to grasp.

Start, therefore, by creating a character or story which you believe will catch the imagination of the paying public, and then look at ways of packaging and selling that product. It may be that a book or a short story is the right first step; it might equally be that a television programme, a film treatment or a radio play would be better starting points.

There is no reason why you shouldn't adapt your creation to suit all these media eventually, but the first step, or first sale, is going to be the hardest, whichever route you choose to take. First get your concept right — you can worry about the quality of your prose later.

10

Selling Non-Fiction Book Concepts to Publishers

Selling non-fiction ideas to publishers is a great deal easier, and can be a great deal more profitable, than selling fictional ones. Publishers are less nervous about buying non-fiction because it is easier for them to influence the final shape of the book, and they can predict more easily what audience it is likely to appeal to.

They also know that even if the author does a sub-standard job, they will probably still be able to render it publishable by editing and rewriting. Consequently, they may be willing to pay you an advance on the book before you have finished writing it – something which only happens to very experienced fiction writers – or even before you have started.

With a work of fiction, publishers are almost completely dependent on the talents of one person – the author. They therefore won't want to risk any money unless they can see the finished manuscript. Non-fiction work, however, can receive input from any number of sources. If you do a truly appalling job, they can even hand the whole project over to someone else, which would be impossible with a work of imagination.

Non-fiction books are therefore likely to make up a major part of any freelance writer's portfolio of work. And although non-fiction writers are not profiled as often in glossy magazines, far more of them can make a decent living from books alone.

Non-fiction is easier for publishers to market, because it is easier to identify the likely readership and target them with advertising and promotional material. For the writer there is the advantage of being able to adapt, update or re-use the material in a number of profitable ways both during and after the book-writing process.

HOW BIG IS THE MARKET?

Imagine, for a moment, creating a book which becomes required reading at universities or specialist colleges around the world, or, better still, a set text in schools. Huge numbers of books will then have to be purchased by the institutions involved, entirely changing the earning potential of a major work.

When you consider all the books used in the educational, or skills-training worlds, coupled with the personal skills and hobby markets (from gardening to football books, from film star biographies to DIY manuals), not to mention reference books and guides on every subject under the sun, you begin to see that the potential market is enormous.

To make a comparison, go to a major bookshop and look at the size of the fiction department. In a large outlet, fiction may account for as little as a quarter of the stock. Having said that, the competition is also very fierce in non-fiction publishing. There are any number of good books available on every subject which has proved popular in the past, so you are still going to have to work hard to make your book the one which people ask for and recommend.

First, however, you have to convince a publishing company that they should pay you to develop your idea. Before they will commit themselves, they need to know that you can give them a product which will sell well for as long a time as possible.

WHAT DO YOU WANT TO WRITE ABOUT?

You need to start off by asking yourself two questions:

1 What do I already know about that might make a book?
2 What do I want to find out about?

The first category might cover your existing work skills, or it might be connected to a hobby or a personal experience. If, for instance, you are a tax expert, you might be able to write a best-seller on how to reduce your tax bills. If you are a keen rose-grower you might be able to write something on that. If you have had a trauma involving illness, death, divorce, or any other experience which afflicts or interests many other people, that too could be useful material for a book.

Since not many of us have more than a couple of potential books in our own heads, and many of us have none at all, most professionally written books come into the second category. They have to be researched. For instance, if you are interested in buying and selling antiques but do not earn a living at it, you will have to go out and talk to people in the business to find out their secrets. If you want to learn to play golf like a professional, or see how women live in the Third World, then you will have to go out and discover the facts for yourself. Once you have satisfied your own curiosity you will be able to pass your knowledge on.

To write this sort of book successfully, you have to 'want' to know the answers. If you are only writing the book because you think there might be a market, and the subject actually bores you, you will have a very unhappy time doing the work, and will probably make an appalling job of it as well. Only if you are truly interested in finding out the answers will you ask the right questions, and only if you are truly excited by the information you manage to collect, will you be able to sustain the effort of writing a complete manuscript.

Books Based on Your Own Experiences

You could write a book based on your experiences of fighting in a war, as the mother of a handicapped child, or as a pop star;

it might be on your memories of fighting drug or alcohol addiction or being held prisoner by terrorists.

However, maybe nothing that interesting, traumatic, meaningful or exciting has happened in your life, so you decide to create an experience to write about. The obvious examples are travel stories, where someone sets off to jog the length of the Great Wall of China, goes round the world in 80 days or makes their way to the South Pole single-handed.

These are extreme examples, and your experience could be of a gentler kind (like buying and doing up a house in France), but the gentler the subject the more skilful the writing will have to be in order to make the story pleasurable and interesting to read.

If you can identify a dream shared by a large number of people − going to live on a desert island perhaps, or moving to a farmhouse in Provence − and then make it come true, there will almost certainly be a readymade audience of people who want to know what it was like, perhaps in the hope that they can one day do the same.

Investigative Books

Then there is investigative writing, where you might infiltrate a sinister organisation or pose as an immigrant worker in a country where they are exploited. George Orwell achieved a mixture of the personal and investigative approaches when he wrote *Down and Out in Paris and London*, which told of his experiences at the poorest end of the social spectrum.

Before undertaking something like this, which could be both hazardous and uncomfortable, you need to be sure that you really want to do it and, more importantly, that there will be a market for the resulting book.

If you are an established writer you may be able to persuade a publisher to commission you before you embark on your journey or experience. Even if they don't come up with any money, they should at least indicate whether or not they think your idea is viable.

In most cases, however, you are going to have to organise and fund the adventure yourself, and hope that you will be able to turn the results into a saleable book. That means you will have to think of other ways to capitalise on the experience while you are looking for a publisher and actually creating the manuscript, such as writing articles or talking on the media (both of which, incidentally, will also help you sell your book to the publishers).

Biographies

There is always a market for biographies of popular or controversial people, as well as historical figures from the past, or the recently deceased. A biography of a controversial film star, athlete, pop singer, criminal or politician can be an enormous potential earner for both a writer and a publisher.

If you approach a publisher with an idea for a biography, the publisher will want to know firstly that you have a genuine enthusiasm for that person and secondly that you have access to information which will give the book a particular selling point. This could be the fact that you have unearthed something no one knew before, or that you have more information than any other writer, or that you have the subject's co-operation.

Biographies range from mighty works on people like George Bernard Shaw and Charles Dickens, which may take anything up to ten years of scholarly research to put together, to paperback biogs of twenty-year-old pop stars, which take a few weeks to research and disappear off the shelves as quickly as the stars disappear off the television screens.

Which end of the market you work on will obviously depend on your personal tastes and abilities, and also on your access to the material. If you are well-known to a number of record companies, have a background in pop music journalism, or know one of the celebrities personally, then you will find it relatively easy to write 50,000 words – or whatever is required – which will appeal to the fans. If you are a sports or political writer, known to the stars and to their friends and families, you will be able to write about them particularly authoritatively, and will know who to approach for help with background information. If you are very well-known within any of these high-profile sectors, you may also be able to get ghostwriting work (see Chapter 16).

There are two schools of thought about whether 'authorised' or 'unauthorised' is the purest form of biography. Publishers will use both words as positive selling points from different angles.

The authorised biography has the blessing of the subject. This suggests that they have given the author more information than would have been available to an unauthorised biographer. On the other hand, it also suggests that the subject has had a say in what can and can't be included. The book may, therefore, appear censored to some readers.

The 'unauthorised' label on a biography suggests either that the subject did not think the writer was of sufficient importance to merit any of their time, or that there is something in the book which the subject would prefer to suppress. It can also mean that a book has been put together hastily from a collection of newspaper cuttings in order to cash in on a sudden surge in the subject's popularity.

Often the only reason stars withhold their co-operation from biographers is because they are hoping to write autobiographies themselves later, and do not want their pitches queered.

The surest way to interest a publisher in an idea for a biography is to be able to demonstrate that you have a personal relationship with the subject, or at least their agreement to co-operate; access to at least one person close to the subject; and access to new and, ideally, controversial information on the subject.

WHERE DO YOU START?

Once you've had your initial idea, on whatever subject, you need to work out what angle you are going to take. The angle might actually be the first thing you think of. For example, because you've had trouble finding a bicycle repair shop in your town, you might decide to write a national guide to bicycle shops. Or, because you always have trouble thinking what to do for children's parties, you decide to write a book containing a hundred children's party ideas.

If, however, you have only decided on the subject and you

don't yet have the angle, you will need to do some research into what is already on the market. The place to start is at your local bookshop. If there are too many other books on the same subject, and you can't think of a sufficiently original angle, then you may have to come up with another idea.

However, just because there is another book available on the same subject, it doesn't mean that other publishers won't be interested in doing something similar. Many of them cover the same areas as their competitors, particularly if they are producing a series of books on a variety of related topics. They will, however, be more interested in an idea which is completely new and won't have to compete with existing titles.

The angle is very important in selling the book at every stage. You need to be able to sum up in one attractive and easily understood sentence what the book is about. Here are some examples:

- 'This book will explain why information technology will change the business world.'
- 'This will tell first-time house buyers all they need to know about buying a home.'
- 'This book will collect the best fashion photographs to come out of Italy during the last fifty years.'

It's not enough just to write a book about information technology, house buying or fashion. You need to focus on the specific aspect you want to cover and the readers at whom you're aiming the book.

On the other hand, the angle needs to be broad enough to appeal to as wide an audience as possible. If you are writing a book about nuclear fusion which will only be understood by a few dozen of the world's greatest scientific brains, don't expect to make much money from it — unless you can persuade each buyer to pay several hundred pounds for their copy.

HOW DO YOU APPROACH PUBLISHERS?

Tell Them About Yourself

To start with, publishers need to know who you are. Are you, for instance, well-known enough in your particular field for people to buy the book simply because it is by you? Are you an established writer with a track record for producing work on time and to brief? Do you have access to the necessary information?

You might have dreamed up a wonderful idea for a new diet book, but a publisher will be much keener on the proposal if you are already an established dietician or, better still, a television exercise teacher.

Tell Them About the Book

They also need to know the answers to the following questions:

- What is the idea for the book?
- Why do you think people will buy it?
- Where will you get the information?
- What other books are there on the subject?

Some publishers are highly scientific about assessing the potential of a book, and will ask you to fill in a questionnaire when you first submit an idea to them. They will ask you detailed questions about the size of the potential market and any trends you may have discerned.

Others will tend to be more governed by hunches and gut reactions. Some authors feel the questionnaire approach is rather daunting, finding it difficult to be so specific at such an early stage, but many others thrive on this sort of detailed and practical approach.

If you have already published one successful book with a publishing house, they are more likely to trust your judgement when you offer them another idea, and might not require you to justify yourself in quite so much detail. However, you will still need to prepare a document which demonstrates that you know what you are talking about, and that there is enough material available to make a book. You may also need to show how your book differs from others on their list which might appear to cover the same areas.

Synopses

The document you prepare should contain a brief synopsis of the book and the potential audience. It should also include a chapter outline – a list of chapter titles with a summary of roughly what will be covered in each one.

The following is a real example of a synopsis that resulted in a published book.

HYPE!
THE ESSENTIAL GUIDE TO MARKETING YOURSELF

How to become high-profile in your industry and exploit fame once you have found it

by
Andrew Crofts

If you can become famous you will be more successful in everything you attempt to do. You will make more money, have more influence over other people and you will enjoy life more.

Being famous increases everyone's earning power dramatically, not only because they can command higher salaries, but because of the extra income to be earned from writing and speaking in public and through the media.

If you can make yourself well-known, people will want to listen to what you have to say. They will be eager to meet you and to hire you. Fame will increase your sphere of influence in your workplace, in your industry and in your social circle.

This book explains how to become well-known in your industry, how to build a wide reputation, and how to use it to climb to the top of the career ladder.

Whether you are a salesman or a lawyer, a grocer or an advertising executive, it helps to be famous – to have a reputation.

This book tells you how to obtain a high profile and how to become known and respected as an expert on your subject. It explains how to get personal publicity in all types of media, from trade magazines to national television, and how to exploit the fame successfully once you have achieved it.

It is a self-improvement book which will be entertaining to read as well as instructive, and will be of interest to ambitious individuals in every walk of life.

SUMMARY OF CONTENTS

1 *Hype Through the Trade Media*
This is the place to start for most people. Either they need to write articles which are published in the right magazines, or they need to persuade the editors and their journalists to interview and quote them. This chapter explains how to make contact with the right editors, how to interest them in what you have to say, and how to write and give interviews.

Pictures are vital for anyone who wants a high profile. Not everyone reads articles in their trade papers, many more glance through the pictures and read the captions. Anyone wanting to promote themselves needs to have a good set of pictures which they can send out with material about themselves. This chapter will also talk about the sort of pictures the media want, and how to go about getting them. It explains how to ensure that your pictures are always the first to come to the art editor's desk when needed.

2 *Hype Through the National Press*
After becoming a spokesperson within your own industry, the next step is to become a spokesperson *for* the industry. That means making sure that the national media know that you are a leading figure in your area; one who is ready and willing to talk when needed, and able to write articles or even regular columns on topical issues. This chapter explains how to gather the right sort of material and how to make the right contacts.

3 *Hype Through Specialisation*
To attain a reputation as an expert in your field, you first have to decide what your field is. The more specialised you

can be the easier it is to carve a niche for yourself. This chapter suggests ways of deciding how to make yourself different from your peer group, and how to ensure that you have the knowledge to back up your ambitions.

4 *Hype Through the Airwaves*
Radio provides another medium for communication and reputation building, as do audio-cassettes (largely for use in the car). The most successful exponents of hype nearly always find a way of packaging their words so that they can work in these media as well. This chapter looks at the available options.

5 *Hype on Stage*
For most business people this means the conference or seminar stage, either appearing as a guest speaker or organising seminars for promotional reasons or for a living. This chapter suggests ways to get on to the public speaking circuit, and looks at some of the techniques for making sure that what you say is remembered and reported in the relevant media (with pictorial coverage). It also suggests ways in which to organise money-making seminars on your chosen subject.

6 *Hype on the Box*
Anyone who appears regularly on television instantly increases their earning power. In the past it has been hard to get there, but with the increase in satellite, cable and video broadcasting, there are numerous ways in which to become a television 'face'. This chapter looks at the available alternatives.

7 *Hype Through Publishing*
Nothing establishes a person's credibility as strongly as having a book published on their chosen subject. This chapter demonstrates how to come up with ideas which will appeal to publishers, and how to present them so that they will be accepted. It also looks at how to exploit the publicity engendered by the launch of the book.

8 *Hype Through Lifestyle*
Some people lead high-profile private lives (Richard Branson, Donald Trump and Malcolm Forbes being obvious examples). At a more modest level, many of the senior people in the advertising industry became famous for the glamour of their homes or cars. This chapter will explain how anyone with an unusual hobby or glamorous lifestyle can make capital from it.

9 *Hype Through Image*
Anyone who is planning to give themselves a high profile needs to be sure that they look the part, and that they are not going to feel disappointed the first time they see themselves on television or in a magazine. That means they have to choose everything to do with their appearance very carefully, from the style of their clothes to the length of their hair, from the shape of their glasses to the sort of jewellery they choose to wear. This chapter will get them to analyse what it is they want to achieve, and what raw materials they have to work with in the first place.

10 *Hype Through Gossip Columns*
Some people manage to use the gossip columns to raise their profiles and show that they are successful. This is largely a question of having the right contacts, although with money or imagination, it is possible for anyone to get gossiped about. This chapter looks at the possible advantages and disadvantages of creating such an image.

11 *Hype Through Scandal*
A scandal can make or break a businessperson. If the chairman of a public company is caught in bed with a page three girl he could either be seen as a 'dirty old man' or as a 'superstud' — it all depends on the way he handles his image and the media. A boardroom takeover battle can take an unknown company into the headlines. The way the protagonists handle themselves can make them famous, or ruin them. This chapter looks at ways to generate controversy that will show you in a good light.

12 *Hype Through Myth and Mystery*

Few people are in a position to use this method — it only works if someone is in a position which automatically makes them objects of curiosity. Instead of talking to the press at every opportunity they shun all personal publicity, and allow stories to build up about them which are neither confirmed nor denied. Charles Saatchi is a good recent example of someone who has shunned publicity and become ever more famous, Howard Hughes at the end of his life was another. This chapter looks at the ways in which people can reach almost legendary status by staying in the shadows and letting people's imaginations do the rest.

THE AUTHOR

Andrew Crofts is an established writer in the areas of management and marketing. He is a regular contributor to many of the leading magazines in both sectors, such as *Marketing Week* and *The Director*, and has authored a number of business books.

He also has extensive experience of the public relations and publicity industries, having worked as a consultant for many of the biggest names in the business.

Sample Chapters

If the publisher already knows your work, a synopsis should be all you need to do. If not, or if this book is very different from others you have done before, you will need to provide a specimen chapter. This will show that you can write and will demonstrate the style you think will suit the subject matter.

If it is a subject you need to research in some depth, it might be hard to produce a sample chapter without understanding the subject in its entirety. In that case it would probably be best to write an introduction which gives an overview of the subject, or to pick one specific element of it and research that.

Bear in mind that you will not be making any money at this stage. In fact you still don't know if you are going to make any money on the project at all. So you want to keep your costs, in terms of time spent researching, as low as possible.

At the same time, you want to find other ways of generating income from the same material. One way is to turn the initial material into articles which you can sell to magazine editors while you are waiting to hear from the publisher. Writing articles on the subject will also help you to see new angles, and to assess from the reactions of editors whether you are on to something interesting or not.

HOW DO YOU MAKE YOUR BOOK SALEABLE?

Once you've convinced the publisher that your idea is good, he or she becomes your champion within the company. They have to want to do the book as much as you do in order to overcome the objections that others on their team might come up with.

The biggest challenge facing your champion is to convince the sales team that they will be able to persuade booksellers to stock your book; or that it can be sold through some other channel such as direct mail. The sales people probably won't meet you personally at this stage − if at all − so you won't be able to convince them with the power of your own arguments. You therefore have to give your champion something they can show the salesforce to explain why the book is a good idea, and why it will be easy to sell.

The document you used to convince the publisher in the first place will not necessarily work on the salesforce, mainly because it is too long.

Draw Up a List of Selling Points

When a publisher's sales person is talking to a buyer from a bookshop, he or she has no more than a few seconds to put across the reasons why they should stock a particular book. So many books are being published and re-published each week that there simply isn't time for them to go into long sales presentations on behalf of your particular offering.

They therefore need to be able to encapsulate the essence of the book in a few easily grasped points. To convince them to buy your idea you need to prepare these selling points for them.

On one side of paper, you should sum up, in bullet form, what the book is about and why it will sell. Your champion can then use this checklist to fight your cause with the sales people. Here are some examples.

GOING FOR A SMALLER BOTTOM

- This is the ultimate diet book, for the part of the body every woman worries about most.
- It gives ten practical exercises which readers can do in the privacy of their own homes.
- The exercises take only ten minutes a day.
- The results are almost immediate.
- The author is a well-known broadcaster and health expert, and willing to give unlimited time to publicising the book.

KINGS AND THEIR MISTRESSES DOWN THE CENTURIES

- This book looks at the women who were the real powers behind the thrones of Europe, some of them scheming and manipulative, others helpless victims of their royal lovers.
- These are true love stories on an epic scale.
- Tales of extraordinary women, some of whom were forced to remain in the shadows, while others were flaunted like prized possessions.
- The book tells of the beautiful palaces built for them, and the extravagant gifts lavished on them.
- It tells how politicians used and abused these illicit liaisons to put pressures on their monarchs.
- The author is an eminent historian, and an accomplished television and radio performer.

Think of a Strong Working Title

It is always helpful to have a strong working title for the book, even if it changes later. The title of any book is like the brand name of a product in a supermarket. It is usually the first thing a potential buyer notices. If it is good it will make them pick it up to see if they want to make a purchase; if it is bad they will pass on to the next one.

A good title doesn't just mean a clever or catchy one, it also needs to be relevant. The title has to tell people exactly what the book is about. For instance, titles that start with simple concepts like 'How to . . .' or '100 Ways to . . .' or 'The Secrets of . . .' can be useful ways to package your ideas in a recognisable form.

This sort of title obeys the first rule of marketing – find out what the customers need and then give it to them. If you can let your readers know in the title which of their needs you are aiming to satisfy you are halfway to making a sale.

Also, when considering any proposal, publishers set great store by whether or not the title grabs their attention, so it is worth putting some thought into it right from the start.

SHOULD YOU APPROACH MORE THAN ONE PUBLISHER?

If you are already a published author, you may be bound by an option clause in your contract to offer your next idea to your existing publisher. Unless things have gone very badly with your first book, it's probably a good idea to do that anyway since you will benefit from already being a known quantity.

If you do not have any such obligation, there is no harm in sending the synopsis out to several relevant publishers at once. The chances of more than one accepting it are very slight, and if more than one does show an interest you will be in the enviable position of being able to ask them to compete for it, either on price or on promises of publicity campaigns.

There are a number of valid reasons why they would reject your idea:

- 'We already have a similar title on our lists.'
- 'We have tried books like this before and have found that they don't work for us.'
- 'The subject area is outside the scope of our publishing plans.'

In many cases the rejection will be an entirely subjective decision, made by one person. The subject, or your treatment of it, simply won't appeal to them.

If you don't spread your net fairly wide, each rejection may take a month or even two months to reach you, and it might be a year after you first thought of the idea that you finally find a home for it.

11

Getting a
Book Written

*A man may write at any time,
if he will set himself doggedly to it.*
SAMUEL JOHNSON, 1750

Many people say they find the thought of sitting down in front
of a blank piece of paper so daunting they seldom manage to
get past it, and could therefore never hope to be writers. If you
find this a problem, then the prospect of writing a book (which
is likely to be at least 70,000 words and could be five times that)
is likely to fill you with more dread than hang-gliding over the
rim of Mount Etna. On the other hand, some writers have
trouble knowing when to stop. Their books gush on for tens of
thousands of words past their expected length, and they feel
sure they have still left a great deal unsaid.

While there are certainly differences between writing fiction
and non-fiction, many of the same problems occur in both.
With fiction, you can't simply 'do some more research' if you
find that your manuscript is falling short of the required
number of words. If you are trying to pad out the length of a
novel it will show in the finished work, and you will find
publishers sending it back.

For most fiction writers, it helps to have the book planned
out from start to finish before they begin to write. Even if you
deviate from your plan as the characters and situations
develop, you need to know roughly what length you are aiming
at, and roughly how long you want each section of the story to

run for. That way you will quickly see if it is running too fast and you can stop and rethink either the plot or the format. It may be that the idea you thought would make a great novel would actually work better as a short story or a play.

MOST BOOKS ARE TOO LONG

There are good reasons why some academic non-fiction books need to go into tremendous detail. There is also a market for 'holiday reading' where works of fiction are used to kill time, so the fatter they are, the better value they represent. But on the whole, I believe that most books could be edited down into long articles or short stories and still tell the readers all they want and need to know about the subject.

However tradition has laid down that, in order to qualify as a book, a piece of writing must be of a certain length, and must be packaged and marketed in a certain way. It is an inefficient and clumsy way of disseminating information in this day and age, but we are all used to it. We tend to trust books more than other media, and part of that trust is probably based on the fact that they are longer and more detailed than articles and pamphlets.

The freelancer should be aware of just how inefficient a system the book is, and should be looking for other ways to sell his or her wares simultaneously. But they also need to prove themselves capable of creating full-length books in order to gain credibility as professional writers. That means learning to find the right number of words to tell your story or explain your ideas.

DEALING WITH WRITER'S BLOCK

Writer's block can be a real problem with a work of fiction, because a writer who has no idea what is going to happen next will have difficulty continuing the story. It is less of a problem with non-fiction, since the facts should carry the story forward for you, if you have assembled enough of them.

I am not saying, however, that there aren't days when it is extremely hard to sit down and write. But if you are going to make a living as a freelance writer you must have a product to sell. It's like being a farmer who doesn't want to spend days ploughing a muddy field, but knows that if he doesn't do it there will be no crops to harvest later in the year. You simply have to do it — if you can't then you won't be able to remain self-employed.

On the days when you don't feel like actually writing, there may be a research or marketing task you can tackle instead. Doing the other task may give you the break you need to refresh you for the next day — just as long as it is something which genuinely needs to be done, and not something you have made up just to get out of doing the writing.

Personally, the only way I find I can overcome writer's block is by writing. That may sound obvious, but anyone who has been in this situation will know what I mean. It doesn't matter if you don't like what you are writing, or if you know that it is sub-standard. The simple act of pouring the words out will unblock the brain. And, sooner or later, some good stuff will begin to flow.

If you find that you are blocked when writing fiction, and you just can't get the plot to move along, try breaking off and writing something about one of the characters. It could be an account of their childhood, schooldays, ambitions, secret vices or anything else. Whatever you write may not form part of the final manuscript, but it will get you thinking about the characters and may lead to new ideas for plot developments. The more you know about your characters' backgrounds the better, and just thinking about something different and writing without worrying about whether the material is good enough for the final manuscript, should help to shift the block.

It is always easier to rewrite, correct and edit than it is to generate original material, particularly with a word-processor. If you spend a day pouring out your thoughts, and another day licking them into shape, you may be travelling at half your best speed, but at least you are still moving forward.

The worst thing you can do is *nothing*, because then you will start to be attacked by guilt and panic. The panic will come from wondering how you are going to support yourself or your family in the future if nothing ever happens to unblock you, and from the knowledge that every day wasted is a day without pay.

The guilt comes from knowing that if you really had to, you could do something about it. I believe that the guilt is the most debilitating factor, if you allow it to go on for too long. At the same time it can also be one of the main motivating factors that makes you get out of bed each morning and sit at your desk.

COLLECTING ENOUGH MATERIAL

If you have never written a book before, it is hard to know how much material you will need. People often say, 'Oh I could write a book about such and such' but in reality most of these ideas and events would probably only contain enough information for a few hundred words. So, before you start writing, you need to collect as much information as possible. Ideally, you will know so much about the subject that you can only fit half of it, or even less, into the final manuscript. That way you will be able to pick and choose the most interesting and relevant parts, and you will not be forced to put in uninteresting material just to pad out the text.

Few professional writers who set out to research a book will have time to gather that much information, but the principle is still the same. There is no point in starting to write until you have an overall feel for the subject, and a mass of data to substantiate your ideas.

SETTING TARGETS

Once you've gathered all your information, you need to divide your subject or story up into as many segments, sections or chapters as possible. It's much easier to write a hundred 400-word pieces than ten 4,000-ones. By tackling the job in bite-sized pieces, one step at a time, you can set yourself realistic targets. The target might be one, five or ten sections a day. Whatever it is, you need to be confident that you will be able to achieve your goal. There is nothing more disheartening than wading into a 10,000-word chunk of text with no clear idea of how you are going to get to the end.

This discipline also helps you to divide the ideas in the book into self-contained articles. Some of these can be lifted out almost untouched, and used as other sources of income or as publicity for the final book (see Chapter 12).

Once the book has been divided into chapters, it helps to list as many bullet points as possible which you want to cover in each chapter. Spend some time on this, because there are always more angles to any subject than are immediately obvious. It might be a good discipline to make yourself think of at least ten for each chapter, or even twenty. You can use the list to check that you haven't forgotten to mention any vital points and it will help you to avoid repetition. It will also force you to think deeply about your subject, and will ensure that you don't start writing until you have enough material to finish. Likewise, if your work on the book is interrupted by other tasks (as it almost certainly will be), your list will help to remind you of which point you have reached in the text.

This system works just as well for fiction as non-fiction. In each chapter you need to know which characters you are going to introduce and what information you are going to give the reader. You also need to know what plot developments you want to reveal at each stage. If you write them down before you start, you will have a structure to follow. When your muse is working well you can forget the structure and let the words flow, but it will still be there for you to go back to when you need it.

In a training or educational book you can incorporate the structure into the actual layout of the text. For instance, you may want to break up every page with subheads, boxes, lists and illustrations, to make the material more accessible. Even if you are writing something where that sort of presentation would be inappropriate − like a biography − you still need to be clear about which points you want to cover when.

GETTING ADVICE

Ask the Experts

If the research for a non-fiction book involves talking to experts, it's always worth asking them what they would like to get from a book of this sort:

- What questions would they like to see answered?
- Where do they think the readers are likely to have gaps in their knowledge?
- Which aspects of the subject do they find most interesting?

Their opinions will give you a clearer idea of how to make the book useful, and whether or not you are on the right lines.

Ask Your Publisher

Inexperienced authors may think they have enough material for a full-length book, only to run dry at 20,000 words. If the book has already been commissioned you are in trouble if you can't find enough words to fulfil your obligations. However if a reputable publisher has commissioned the book, they are probably confident that there is enough material available, so it may just be a question of going out to look for it.

If this happens to you, it may be worth printing out the 20,000 words, sending it to your publisher as a first draft, and asking which areas they think need to be developed. They will welcome the opportunity to see how their investment is coming along, and should be able to suggest ways in which you can expand on what you have already written.

A LAST WORD OF ADVICE

Before you send your manuscript off, be sure to read it through at least once from beginning to end, to check that it flows and makes sense, and that you haven't missed anything out or repeated yourself.

The hardest thing when starting a book is to convince yourself that you will ever reach the end. The only way to get there is with small steps.

12

Marketing a Book

Many writers believe that their job is to create the book and it is then up to the publisher to market it. All they are willing to do is make themselves available for media interviews with anyone the publisher manages to nobble.

It's true that publishers have marketing departments whose job is to sell as many books as possible in any way they can think of. If your book is destined to be a best-seller, or if it is, say, an educational book, with a captive market, you may be able to leave it up to your publisher, confident that there is nothing you need do to supplement their efforts. In most cases, however, you will have to provide AT LEAST HALF of the marketing driving force if your book is to be successful.

Most books are likely to earn only small amounts of money for the publishers. While their publicity departments will try to get your work reviewed and to get you interviewed by the media at the time of publication, within a couple of weeks several more products will be coming off their assembly line, and they won't have any time left to devote to yours. From then on, they will be largely reactive, responding to any requests which come from the media, but not going out in search of opportunities.

For most books this level of marketing is not going to sell enough copies to make a reasonable financial return for the author. As already discussed, books are seldom big earners for writers anyway. They can, however, act as loss-leaders. The more high-profile a book is, the more helpful it will be in getting you commissions for other projects. Almost as a by-product of this success you will also sell more copies of the book itself.

So it is definitely worth helping to market your book. In many cases it is more important that people hear about the book than that they actually buy it. Also, if you help to promote your own book it will encourage the publisher to keep trying.

To sell well, your book has to be marketed successfully to both the book trade and the reader. The latter is the most important, because if potential readers are coming in asking for the book the shops will be happy to order it for them. If you manage to convince the shops to stock the books, but you don't convince the public to buy them, you are going to end up with a lot of unsold books being returned to your publisher.

SELLING TO THE BOOK TRADE

It is easier, however, to market to the book trade than to the general public, because there are a limited number of people to talk to, and they can be reached through a relatively small number of media.

The publisher will do most of the work on the trade, which will mean sending out catalogues, possibly advertising in book trade magazines, and getting their sales team to sell the book to the booksellers. The author can help by agreeing to do book signings or anything the shops ask for.

If the book trade can be convinced that your book is going to sell well, they will stock more copies and display them more prominently, and that will help to raise awareness amongst potential customers, although it won't necessarily make them buy.

One way to convince the shops that people will want to buy the book is by demonstrating that there is going to be a lot of publicity, in the form of advertising, reviews or public relations activities which will stimulate customers to come into the shops asking for the book.

The chances are, however, that the publisher's budget won't allow for any significant consumer advertising, and you will be relying mainly on other sorts of publicity to bring the book to the attention of potential buyers.

SELLING TO THE READER

Until the moment of acceptance all your efforts have been directed towards selling your work to a publisher. It is like the manufacturer of a new drink working hard to get it accepted on to the shelves of a major supermarket chain. Once it is on the shelves, the manufacturer has to tell potential customers that the drink exists and persuade them to purchase it as well as, or in preference to, competing products.

However the manufacturer of the new drink probably has the advantage of a huge advertising, promotional and merchandising budget. By contrast, publishers occasionally assign some money to advertising specific books, but only enough to buy a few small ads in a couple of relevant magazines. Sometimes potential best-sellers fare a little better, but we are still talking about relatively small amounts of money compared to the vast sums lavished on products like soap powder.

The reason is obvious. Even with a huge advertising budget, the number of people who will actually buy the book is a great deal smaller than the number who will buy a packet of soap powder. On top of that they will only buy it once, whereas they could go on buying soap powder every other week for the rest of their lives.

You could argue that by spending a lot on promoting one book by an author, a publisher is building a brand awareness which will make it easier to sell the rest of his or her books later on. This may be true, but writers are not as reliable as soap powder or Japanese cars. They do not always stay in their packets when they are told to, and they do not always perform consistently. Publishers are very nervous about investing a lot of money in authors, only to find that they move to other publishers with their next books, never produce anything worth reading again, or start writing about something which appeals to a completely different segment of the market.

For all these reasons there will be a very small advertising budget, and most of the promotional effort will go into public relations activities, which by and large means free plugs in newspapers and magazines, or on radio and television.

So what makes people want to buy your book? There are three main types of buyer you need to consider:

1 *The Buyer with a Purpose*

These buyers want or need to learn about a subject, and consequently go into their nearest bookshop and buy whatever is available.

In this case you have to make sure that your book is in the shop when they come in, and that it looks better than the competition. Both these factors are largely up to the publisher's design and distribution departments, but you should bear this type of buyer in mind when making all the early decisions on how to write and present the book.

2 *The Browser*

These buyers come into a shop to browse. They probably intend to buy something to read, but have nothing particular in mind. If they spot your book they will buy it.

The odds against them spotting your book are heavy – bear in mind how many books there are in any one shop. Unless your book is positioned very prominently, it is unlikely to stand out from the crowd.

3 *The Buyer Who Seeks You Out*

These customers have heard of your book – either through the media or through word of mouth – and they have decided to seek it out. The only thing that will stop them buying is if your book isn't there, or if there is something else on the shelf which they prefer.

If it isn't on the shelf they can ask the shop to order it for them. This is a major barrier to purchase for many who are not prepared to wait. It will not stop the determined ones but if they find something they prefer, there is little you can do. These are the customers the author has the power to create and encourage.

HOW CAN YOU HELP TO MARKET YOUR BOOK?

Recommend Reviewers

Most publishers will be very happy to send review copies of the book to any journalist or broadcaster who shows the slightest interest. So if you have had any dealings with anyone in the media, or know of any critics or journalists who may be particularly interested in the subject of your book, you should give their names to the publisher.

Unless there is someone specific to send the book to, i.e. someone you or the publisher knows by name, there is no telling who will end up taking the book home. Often the publisher will send out a review copy and phone the magazine a few weeks later to find out if it has been received, only to find that no one knows anything about it.

Good reviews are the best possible sort of word-of-mouth promotion, and they undoubtedly help to sell a book off the shelves or through direct mail. But unfortunately there aren't that many publications which give much space to book reviews, and those that do are as likely to say something bad or dismissive about your efforts as they are to praise them. (In fact, as a bad review is usually more entertaining to write and to read, they are more likely to be negative than positive.) So you cannot rely on this source of publicity alone.

Encourage Other Word-of-Mouth Recommendations

The best way to make a book popular is by word of mouth. The only way to get word-of-mouth working is to convince a core of people to read your book in the first place, so that they can start recommending it to others. The more influential those people are, the quicker the word will spread.

Give your publishers a list of the names and addresses of any relevant individuals. Publishers are reluctant to send out free books on a whim, so select your potential words of mouthers carefully, and be prepared to explain why you think they should be sent a copy.

Approach Magazine Editors

Writing a magazine article on the subject of your book is an excellent way of promoting it. In order to get a magazine editor interested, you need to go back to the original synopsis you used to sell the book to the publisher.

Check that the angles are still relevant, and that you haven't changed your opinions while writing the book. Then work out which media are likely to be interested in which aspects, and pick A MAXIMUM OF TWO ANGLES for each publication.

An angle might be the overall concept for the book, or it might be one specific idea from one chapter. It doesn't matter which it is as long as it can be summed up in one short paragraph and it will definitely be of interest to readers of that particular publication.

Before you start contacting magazine editors, send a letter to the publicity director at your publishers, explaining who you plan to approach and what you intend to offer them. It is possible that the publishers are hoping to sell serialisation rights of the book to a particular editor and you might jeopardise that sale by offering an article at a much lower price – or free. In most cases, however, the publishers will be delighted with any efforts you put in to publicise your work.

About three months before publication of the book, start writing to the editors of monthly and weekly magazines. Then about a month before publication, write to the national, local and daily press, if the subject is relevant to them. Once you have caught their attention, you can then offer them a choice of other, more specific angles, if they aren't sure about the one you have sent.

If a book is of specialist interest, make sure it goes to the editor or correspondent who covers that subject. If you have written a new book on computers there is no point sending it to the literary editor of a newspaper, but the technology or computing correspondents might well be interested in your ideas, and might give them coverage, mentioning the book as a source.

The following letter was sent to the editors of management, marketing, communications and television magazines before the publication of a book on business television:

Dear Mr. Smith,

USING TELEVISION AND VIDEO IN BUSINESS

I have written a book with the above title, which is being published by Mercury Books in the Spring. The main contention of the book is that television and video will soon become as commonplace within the business world as the telephone and the personal computer.

It looks at all the different uses of television, from private networks to video-conferencing, interactive training to corporate videos, animation to sponsored television. It talks about what is happening now and how companies should ensure that they are not left behind.

Would you be interested in an article, either taking an overview of the situation or looking at one aspect of it which might be particularly relevant to your readers, or tailored to fit into a special feature you might be planning?

Yours sincerely,

Andrew Crofts

A number of magazines asked for an article directly from the letter, while some asked for more details of the content of the book, and for a few suggestions of different angles which would suit their readers.

The following letter was a response to the editor of a marketing magazine who wanted a selection of angles to choose from:

Dear Mr Smith,

As promised, may I suggest some possible topics for articles around the theme of 'Using Television and Video in Business'.

1 Soon managers will be appearing on television as often as they talk on the phone or tap into a personal computer. What will that mean to their daily working lives and how should they be preparing themselves? (i.e. How can they become effective broadcasters and why will it be necessary to master these skills?)

2 Will business television replace business travel and the old-fashioned face-to-face meeting? How can television technology be used to take conferences down the line, to avoid the cost of moving people to one central location?

3 How to commission a corporate video – and avoid wasting your money.

4 Everyday business television activities will soon include sponsored broadcast programmes as well as private corporate networks and video conferencing facilities – how can companies ensure that they use the whole mix effectively?

5 Ways in which business television can be used effectively and imaginatively as an aid to sales calls or at point of sale.

Would any of these fit in with your plans?

Yours sincerely,

Andrew Crofts

In the end this particular editor picked out elements of two of the suggestions and asked to have them amalgamated into one article.

A month later another letter went out to the media editors and consumer editors of the national daily and Sunday papers:

Dear Mr Smith,

WITHIN TEN YEARS COMMUNICATING VIA TELE-
VISION WILL BE AS COMMONPLACE AS COMMUNI-
CATING BY TELEPHONE OR COMPUTER

This is the concept behind a book I have written called
Using Television and Video in Business which is being
published on 29 April by Mercury Books.

The book explains how telecommunications, television
and computer technologies are coming together to create
opportunities like private corporate television networks and
video-conferencing facilities.

In this century the telephone gave us the ability to talk to
anyone we chose, anywhere in the world, whenever we
chose. In the next century television will take it all a step
further, cutting out much of the need for long-distance
travel and making the 'global village' a reality.

Do you think your readers would be interested in a
feature on this subject, explaining what the changes are
likely to mean to them?

Yours sincerely,

Andrew Crofts

Write a Master Article

Even before you have had a response from the editors, it's worth
preparing a master article which sums up the main contentions
or storyline of the book in around 1,000 words.

This exercise will help to clarify your idea of exactly what the
key message of the book is. It will give you a skeleton which you
can quickly adapt and build up into other articles when you get
specific requests back from editors. And it will give you
something to send editors on a speculative basis, showing how
an angle would work in practice.

Sometimes an article sent in speculatively will result in an
editor asking for a different angle and rejecting the actual
article you have sent. Or, better still, they may follow up the
idea in order to write about it themselves, using you and your
book as a source of quotes.

131

This gives you a double benefit since it allows you to send your master article on to someone else, while also getting objective coverage in your first choice of publication.

Furthermore you may end up earning more from these articles than the advance you received from the publishers for the whole book. By researching a book you have built up a store of knowledge and formulated ideas which you can then sell on in other forms.

However not all the editors will feel that they should pay for your pieces, believing that free publicity for the book is reward enough. On the whole, editors who feel like this will be from the smaller and poorer publications. But presumably they have access to an audience which you want to target for the book. You will therefore have to weigh up whether it is worth doing the piece for nothing -- usually it is.

The fact that they are receiving the article for free will oblige them to promote the book more strongly than they would if they were paying you the going journalistic rate – but you still won't be able to promote the book as blatantly as you would in an advertisement.

If you keep gratuitously mentioning the book in the text of an article any editor is going to take the mentions out, or reject the article completely. You may, however, be able to work in a mention in three different places.

The most common place is at the foot of the article where they will carry a small italicised announcement that you are the author of a book on ..., and if you are lucky they will also name the publisher, the price of the book and the date of publication, if relevant.

If the editor is feeling particularly kindly disposed towards you, they may even include a 'reader enquiry number'. These are systems whereby readers can send requests in to magazines to obtain more information about something they have read. The magazine then sends the enquirer's name and address on to your publisher, who can sell them a book.

Next, you could get the book mentioned in the subhead introducing the article – 'by Andrew Crofts, author of the recently published ...'

Thirdly you might get it mentioned in a picture caption. The picture might be of you, as the author of the article, or of the cover of the book if it is photogenic. Mentions in captions are important since many people who scan through magazines without reading the articles will still glance at the pictures.

You won't get any of these mentions, however, UNLESS YOU INCLUDE THEM WITH YOUR SUBMISSION.

Approach Radio and Television Producers

Your publisher's marketing department will approach the obvious television and radio producers who might be interested in your book at the time of publication, but that doesn't mean that you can't approach them yourself from a different angle.

Local radio and, to a lesser extent, local television stations always like to find people from their area who have something interesting to talk about. Authors of books make good subjects.

Simply writing to tell them that you are publishing a book might get you some response, but it would be better still if you could suggest specific angles from the book which you could talk about, just as you did for the magazines and newspapers. If you can think of a way in which the idea can be built up into a controversy, with people of opposing views being invited into the studio to debate with you, all the better.

Many regional and local radio stations also like to interview people who are not local but have something of interest to say. It's always worth getting on the air anywhere that the book is going to be on sale, but it may not always be worth travelling to do it in person. Most of the stations will be happy to interview someone over the telephone, or, if they are part of a national network, from one of their studios in a major city. They won't expect you to travel miles in order to talk to them for five minutes.

Do a Promotional Tour

Your publishers may decide to arrange a promotional tour for you. They are only likely to do this if you or your book are of considerable interest to the general public. Otherwise it will not be worth their while investing in so much administration, and not worth your while investing that much time.

A tour will include talking to local journalists and radio stations in each town you go to, and going in to bookshops for signing sessions or simply to meet the staff. This all helps to raise awareness of your name and the name of the book, and if the publishers are willing to put their time and money into organising such a tour, it's worth your while co-operating.

If your publishers aren't planning anything like this, but you think this sort of exposure will help sales of your book, it might be worth organising a tour of your own. You should then make contact with all the local newspapers and radio stations to tell them you are going to be in their area, and make contact with the bookshops through your publisher.

However most books do not merit this sort of campaign, and will not gain much more coverage than if all the promotion had been done by letter and telephone.

Keep the Publicity Going

Publicity is rather like a fire. It can be very hard to get it to light in the first place. But once the flames have taken hold, it will spread of its own volition. Once a story has been published or broadcast in one of the national daily papers or you have been interviewed on national radio or television, other media will follow it up.

The chances are that you will then be swamped by requests from other papers and radio stations for interviews. Many of those people who have been suddenly triggered into life may have had press releases and even review copies at the same time and failed to act on them. Perhaps they just didn't notice them, or failed to see how the angle would work for a general audience. Whatever the reason for the initial lethargy, a good article demonstrating how the story will work, will stimulate other media to respond.

Because of the efforts of your publisher — as well as your own first round of approaches — there will be a flurry of activity at the time of publication. The publisher's publicity department will then have to move on to other books. You, however, must continue to concentrate on your own project.

Keep circulating your articles to the relevant media, changing the angles and sending them out in rotation. You are as likely to achieve a breakthrough in the form of major exposure a year after the book is published as you are at the time of publication. Secondary media will be just as ready to pick up on a good story which doesn't coincide with a publication date as one which does.

Sell Other Rights

Marketing a book also involves selling subsidiary rights, for things like foreign translation, television and film, or serialisation in a magazine or newspaper.

Sales of foreign rights may include other English-speaking territories like the USA, where the potential readership is vast and consequently the payments can be relatively more generous. Then there are foreign translations, which are initially less profitable because the publishers have to pay for the translators' fees, but may bring in useful amounts in the long term.

In most cases the publishers will handle these sorts of sales for you. However if you think you stand a better chance of success than they do, insist on retaining whatever rights you want when you first sell them the book.

Most inexperienced writers are not equipped to handle these sorts of negotiations personally, and it would be wise to get an agent to help with all the adjustments to contracts and with the actual selling of subsidiary rights (see Chapter 17).

Think About Other Ways of Selling the Book

There may be organisations who would benefit from the wider distribution of your book. If, for instance, you have written something about historic buildings, tourism and heritage organisations might have a vested interest in helping to promote it, as might the owners of the buildings and the travel suppliers who bring people to them. If you have written a book about healthy eating, there may be manufacturers who provide the sort of food you have talked about who would be interested in seeing the book reach a wider audience.

You could alert your publisher's marketing department to these possibilities, giving them whatever contact names and details you have, or you could follow them up yourself initially, and then put them in touch with the publisher once you have interested them in an offer of some sort. For instance, a particular trade magazine might want do so some sort of joint promotion, giving copies of the book away to their readers, or selling them at a preferential price.

13

Writing for
the Business World

The worlds of business and industry have an endless need for words because they have to communicate with so many different audiences:

- They need to market their goods to customers.
- They need to explain themselves to their employees and to their shareholders.
- They need to supply information to the media, to politicians, to pressure groups and to their peer groups.

In order to perform these tasks effectively, they have to be clear in their thinking and skilful in their writing. They also need to have a great deal of time. Fortunately for us, they are always short of time, and often short on the other two requirements as well.

As well as availability of work, the immediate financial rewards for corporate work are substantially better than for most other writing jobs. (For more on comparative rates of pay, see Chapter 20.)

WHAT ARE THE POTENTIAL OUTLETS?

Trade Papers

Trade papers always need good editorial from professional writers. If they can get it free from companies they will be even happier, provided the material is written well and objectively enough to satisfy their editorial standards.

If the companies can get their points of view published in the trade papers, then they too are very happy. The companies therefore need to find people who can write to sufficiently professional standards for their work to be accepted by magazine editors. These writers also have to understand and sympathise with the messages the companies are trying to convey.

In-House Magazines

These might be written for staff or customers, or for the outside world. The aim is always to put across the company's point of view and image, but in-house magazines have to be written sufficiently well and objectively to be attractive to potential readers. Company magazines are increasingly coming to resemble consumer publications and they need writers who can perform to those standards.

Brochures

Most companies need sales literature of some sort, whether they are selling financial services or brass screws, and it has to be written so that it can be easily understood. The people working within the companies are often too close to the products to be able to explain them objectively so they may need the help of outside writers.

Annual Reports

Increasingly, companies want their annual reports to work as marketing tools for them, which means they have to explain clearly and convincingly what they have been doing in the past ·

138

year and what they intend to do in the future. A writer can help them do this.

Speeches

Managers are frequently called upon to make speeches. They usually know what their key messages should be, but they can't see how to string them together convincingly and make the results flow. They don't have time to lavish the necessary care and attention on their speeches, so they may well call on the services of a professional writer.

Press Releases

Companies who want to be reported accurately in the media will issue press releases on any new internal developments. Writers can help make the information more succinct and more relevant to the editors, although it would probably not be practical for a freelancer to do press releases only for a client. However if a writer is already familiar with a company because of other in-depth writing work they can easily adapt the material for press releases.

Video Scripts

The increasing use of television as a business communication medium means that there is a growing market for business television scripts, just as there is for broadcast television. Once again, it is important to be able to understand the needs of the sponsoring company as well as the needs of the television production people and the final audience.

Letters

Some companies even need help with composing letters, particularly if they are selling letters which are going to be sent out to dozens, hundreds or even thousands of prospective customers.

WHO DO YOU APPROACH?

The Professional Advisers

The first people to approach are the professional advisers who help companies with their words – i.e. public relations consultancies and editorial companies producing in-house magazines on contract. Most of these operations will be staffed by people who have some writing skills and experience. However they won't always be equipped for a sudden rush of work, and it is when an emergency job comes up that they will generally call in freelancers.

In-House Public Relations Departments

These are less fertile hunting grounds for the freelancer since they are generally working under less pressure. Also, in-house public relations people generally have a deeper understanding of the company's products and are therefore able to write more of the material themselves.

Once a public relations department does start using a freelancer, however, they are likely to stick with them because of the inside knowledge the freelancer will have built up in the course of their research. It is always preferable for a company to use someone they won't have to brief from scratch for every job, since it is in the briefing that the most time can be wasted.

Other In-House Staff

Public relations managers and directors aren't the only people within companies who might need the services of writers, although they are probably the most frequent users. Large companies might have a publications manager or an editor whose sole job is to produce in-house literature. Personnel managers might also want writers to present employee information. And managers in any department may need help with writing a report or a speech. Finally, sales and marketing departments could need writers to help with their material.

How Do You Find These People?

There are public relations consultancies everywhere, although the majority of them are concentrated in the major cities. The books listing them should be available in most reference libraries (see the 'Directories ' section under Useful Addresses).

In-house public relations people are harder to find, simply because there are so many of them. The best approach is to decide which industry sectors you would like to work in and have some experience of. For instance, if you have been writing articles for a personal finance magazine, which has involved you in talking to several finance companies, you should approach these companies first with samples of your published work from the magazine which you hope they will recognise and find impressive.

Lists of companies can be found in libraries, and most industries have associations and institutes which publish reference works about their members, keep reference libraries, or would be able to advise you on where to go for the necessary information.

How Do You Sell Your Services to Them?

The way to get this sort of work is to make sure that your name is on the right person's desk at the moment when a crisis hits them. Whenever I have been given a business writing job by someone I have not worked for before, they nearly always say something like: 'Your letter arrived on my desk at exactly the right time.'

There is no way you can judge when that right time will be. You just have to keep sending out letters and promotional materials. The idea is to give yourself as high a chance as possible of landing on the right desk at the right time, while guarding against pestering people too often.

Eventually you can create a network of contacts who have your name in their address books and come back to you whenever they need a writer. But you will still have to replenish this network regularly, replacing people who move up and no longer commission writers or move out of the industry altogether.

There are a number of ways in which you can reach new business customers with your sales message:

- You could advertise in professional marketing magazines (see Useful Addresses) but that would be expensive, with no guarantee of success.
- You could maintain a steady flow of direct mail letters explaining who you are and what your speciality is.
- You could prepare a brochure or leaflet about yourself, or simply send a letter.
- You could send samples of your work.
- You could phone them and sell yourself verbally.

Whatever method you choose, you have to make them understand immediately what services you are selling and convince them that they should keep your name on file for the time when an emergency hits them.

THE DRAWBACKS OF BUSINESS WRITING

They Have the Final Say

Although magazine editors and book publishers have the final say in what they print, they are quite likely to bow to your opinion in confrontation. If you want your book to be written in a certain style, or you want your article to take a certain angle, they will be willing to take your arguments on board and may even give you theirs in a reasoned fashion. If you reach an impasse, and you don't want to do it their way, you can always give them back their money and take your work elsewhere.

Business clients have no such scruples. They are paying you to perform a service for them, just as they would pay an accountant to audit their finances or a lawyer to fight their case in court. If they respect your abilities they will certainly listen to your advice but in the end they can demand that a piece is written the way they want.

If you feel that this compromises you in some way — for

instance, if they want you to write an article which makes patently false claims for their products — then you can refuse to do the work. But you will then be out of pocket since you can't sell the work to anyone else.

Alternatively, you could refuse to have your name attached to the piece. In most cases you will have been writing anonymously anyway, but it is possible that the company has hired you because your name is well known in their industry, and they will be willing to make compromises to keep your valuable byline.

Office Politics

The fact that the public relations manager likes your piece doesn't mean that everyone else will. The person who commissions you to do the work will almost certainly have to report to someone else, and your copy will end up being vetted by any number of people before being printed or circulated to a wider audience.

There is a golden rule in the world of writing: If someone is sent something to check, they will always feel obliged to change it. If you use the word 'large' they will change it to 'big'. Rest assured that had you chosen the word 'big' in the first place, the same person would have changed it to 'large'.

If a piece therefore has to be approved by a team of people, you are going to have to accept that a great many changes will be made, and the resulting work may not be as strong as it was when you first wrote it. It is also possible, however, that you will learn a great deal from other people's comments — they may even improve on what you have done.

Just make sure that when you quote for the job you take into account the fact that you may have to attend meetings and produce rewrites weeks or even months after you were first commissioned to do the job.

143

14

Writing for Stage, Screen and Radio

This way lies as much potential for wasted time and heartache as in the quest to publish a novel. It is an area crammed with hopefuls, all turning out lengthy scripts which then have to be submitted to a few overworked and very cynical potential customers. The slush piles of unsolicited scripts in major film and television companies are just as massive as in major book publishers, and just as many of them are rejected.

On the whole, it is a waste of time to write an entire script for any performance medium in the hope that it will sell. So much professional work has to go into creating a final script for shooting or staging, that it will generally bear little or no resemblance to the first draft anyway.

Any writer who doesn't intend to act as the producer for his or her own work is going to have to find a collaborator within the chosen medium. That collaborator or champion could be a producer, a studio executive, a director, an agent or even a well-known actor in search of a vehicle. Whatever happens, someone else has to help get the idea to the stage where someone will provide the money to turn it into a film, play or television programme.

Your first step therefore is to win that ally. Most of these people are extremely busy and have a great many approaches made to them every week. You therefore have to work very hard to catch their attention and sell them your idea.

PRESENTING AN IDEA

The idea may exist in the form of a short story, a novel which you have already had published, a setting for a soap opera or a synopsis for a play or film which has sprung freshly into your mind. But it still needs to be distilled down to its essence, a short, tightly written synopsis which clearly demonstrates why it would be suited to that medium.

If you can't get someone to 'buy' your idea you are never going to get them to 'buy' a completed script – so why waste your time writing the whole thing straight away? By making the synopsis as attractive as possible you are also preparing the ground for the final product. The more work you do at this preliminary stage, whether you are creating a television game show, a documentary or a Hollywood blockbuster, the better the final product is likely to be, and the better your chances of selling it.

Just like book publishers, the people you are selling this concept to need to be able to see immediately how they will be able to sell it on to other people. They have to be able to persuade their colleagues to share their enthusiasm for it, financiers to back it and the public to go and see it. They also need to persuade busy directors and stars to be involved in the project. It's no good being deep or esoteric at this stage. There are too many good ideas around for anyone to waste time trying to work out what you are trying to get at.

Some great original screenplays could not have been explained convincingly to a producer in synopsis form, but not enough to make it a gamble worth taking. If you are already well connected, with a string of successful films or plays to your credit, then you may be able to get potential customers to read complete screenplays. But even then it's still a good idea to judge the reactions you are likely to get and adjust your ideas accordingly.

If you truly don't believe that your idea will be convincing in synopsis form, it might be better to try writing it first in the form of a short story or novel, and then sell the film rights later.

PREPARING A SAMPLE SCRIPT

There are some areas, such as comedy, where you have to show potential buyers the actual product in order to convince them that it is worth buying. No one is going to invest in a comedy sketch or series until they are sure that it is funny.

Even so, you should write a synopsis first describing roughly what the setting for the comedy is, to see whether they would be interested in seeing anything further. For instance, you may want to write a comedy series about a marine biologist and that particular television station may know that it would never buy such a thing, either because they have already done something similar, or because they couldn't afford to shoot all the location scenes or because they know that it wouldn't fit into their schedules.

It's possible that you will have to write at least one full script to show anyone who takes an interest how the idea will work, but if no one wants to take it any further you might as well save your time. (For advice on how to present scripts, see the books listed under 'Writing for Film, Television and Radio' in the Bibliography.)

ADAPTING YOUR IDEA

If you have a good idea for a film, ask yourself if the same idea wouldn't work just as well on stage or television or radio. Why limit your potential sales by aiming at only one medium?

When you prepare your synopsis, do as many versions as you can − one for film, one for television (although these two are increasingly overlapping), another for radio and another for the stage. There is no reason why you should stop there. For instance, the idea might work as a one-off television play or as a series, as a fringe theatre production or as a major West End show.

If you can adapt your idea as a fringe show which can be produced — perhaps even by yourself or by friends — at very little cost, you have increased the chances of it becoming a reality. Once it is staged as a fringe production, you will have a chance to develop it in conjunction with the performers and the director, and you will be able to test the reactions of audiences. If the idea is strong enough, it will then be easier to adapt for a larger theatre and a wider audience. You can invite potential producers to see the play itself (rather than just a script), and explain how it would be adapted.

If the play proves to be a success in a major theatre, you can adapt it again to attract a film producer, and so on. It is much more likely that you will be able to climb the ladder of success in this way, than that you will be able to hurtle straight on to the big screen or the Broadway stage.

There are also less well-known outlets for performance writing, such as business training videos. If you have written a book on effective selling techniques, a video production house might turn it into a programme which could be marketed alongside the book. Similarly, a children's story might lend itself to adaptation on to tape, so that children could listen to it in the car or at home.

Look at every possible alternative and produce a synopsis to fit each one. Then start sending them round with covering letters to the relevant buyers.

If you have the time, there is no reason why you shouldn't start work on a full script if you are burning to get on with it, but it would make more sense to wait. If no one shows the remotest interest in your synopses, you will know that any further work you do on the project will have to be for your own satisfaction, not because you are likely to make a sale.

SELLING ON EXISTING PROJECTS

You may have already written fiction or non-fiction books, short stories or articles which would make good films or television programmes. Sometimes the film or television people will approach you and offer to buy the rights to use your work in their media, or your publishers will sell the rights on your behalf, but you can't rely on that happening. On the whole, it is up to you to sell the idea of the adaptation.

If, when you sell a book to a publisher, you think there is a good chance that it will convert for other media, you should consider retaining the film and dramatic rights so that you can sell them yourself. This is where an agent can help (see Chapter 17), in negotiating the contract with the publisher and selling the rights to a producer.

SELLING OPTIONS

Options are wonderful things, because you can just keep on selling them. They are also frustrating because they don't always mean that a project will reach fruition.

What happens is that you offer an idea, a book or a script for sale. A producer likes it but doesn't want to buy it outright in case he can't raise the money needed to make it. He therefore offers to buy the option for six months to a year, at the end of which time he should know whether he can raise the money and make a bid for the whole thing.

If he still isn't sure whether the deal will work at the end of that period, he can renew the option for a further six months or a year. If he decides not to renew, you are then free to offer it to other people again. A great many properties that never get made into actual films earn option fees for their authors for years.

Obviously, it is frustrating to think that your work is going to be made into a film and then find that the options go dragging on, but that is the nature of film and television anyway, and it is much better to be paid while you wait than to receive nothing.

If you have written an entire script, the option fees will seem a less than generous return on time invested. If, however, you have merely put together a synopsis they are an extremely profitable sideline.

BRINGING IN OTHER WRITERS

The fact that someone has bought the rights to film your book or idea does not necessarily mean that you will be asked to write the final script. The producer may have a writer they always like to use, or they may not like your style. Equally, they might ask you to write the first draft and then hand that on to others for rewriting.

Although it is obviously disappointing not to be involved in the project from start to finish, there are considerable advantages to being paid for a product which you need do no more work on.

THINKING ABOUT THE SIDE EFFECTS

There can be enormously beneficial side effects for any project which is adapted for other media. A book which is made into a film is likely to sell far more copies when it is re-released to coincide with the movie. Likewise, a documentary springing from the material in a book will draw attention to the content and help to sell more copies.

The aim for a writer is to sell his or her ideas to as many different media as possible. Then the exposure provided by one medium will help to ensure success in the others. It is easier to sell the film rights to a best-selling book than an unpublished synopsis. It is easier to convince publishers to accept a book based on a successful television series than one which is wholly original . . . And so the circle continues.

15

Travel Writing

One of the great advantages of being freelance is having the freedom to travel wherever and whenever you choose. The only limitation is financial. However if you can ensure that you are earning money while you travel, and if you can find other people who will be willing to pay for expenses such as flights, accommodation and car hire, then even that limitation is eradicated.

To persuade other people to support you in this way you must become an international writer, bringing home stories from all over the world for English-speaking publications everywhere. (If you are able to contribute to publications in other languages too, so much the better.)

The most common form of international writing is in the travel industry, but it is by no means limited to that. If your speciality is the building industry, for instance, you could be reporting on dam-building projects in Holland, skyscrapers in Hong Kong or hotel complexes in Honolulu. If you write about agricultural subjects you could be studying farming methods in the Third World or food production on the Russian Steppes. For the sake of simplicity, however, I'll refer to all these activities as 'travel writing'.

WHY TRAVEL?

There are three reasons why any freelance writer should consider doing some travel writing. The first is the sheer pleasure of doing it, the excitement of visiting places and enjoying experiences which you might otherwise never come across.

The second reason is that the further you cast your net in search of material, the more likely you are to find good and interesting stories, and the wider your perspective will become. 'Travel broadens the mind' is a cliché, but for a writer who wants to gain an understanding of the world it is indisputably true.

The third reason is that it will increase your professional standing, demonstrating to potential customers that you are capable of seeking out stories wherever they are, and that you have a wide experience of the world.

WHERE SHOULD YOU GO?

You can go virtually anywhere, though it might be best to avoid areas which are actually at war (unless that is the subject you want to cover). So you need to work out firstly where you would most like to go, and secondly where you are likely to find the sort of material your customers want.

For instance if you write on religious topics you need to go to a country which provides interesting material for articles or books on theological thought and religious rituals. It could be the Vatican City or the voodoo worshippers of Haiti; it might be a visit to a religious carnival in Rio or a monastery in the Tibetan mountains.

If cookery is your subject then you can go almost anywhere, although you are more likely to find unusual dishes to describe in South America or Burma than you are in France or Italy, where food writers have been travelling for centuries.

Alternatively, if you write about business and marketing subjects then Hong Kong, Tokyo or New York are likely to prove fruitful for international business stories, and the conference and incentive facilities of the Caribbean or South Pacific will provide a wealth of raw material for special features in trade magazines.

If possible, you will be finding material on a number of different subjects wherever you go, but you should start with the sector where you already have a track record, in order to convince editors and publishers, and the people who can provide travel facilities, that you are worth investing in.

To a degree then, your first choice of destination will be guided by your interests and your current contacts. You might want to set off immediately for Tahiti or Rio, but you may have to start with Dusseldorf or Brussels in order to build up your contacts and credibility.

WHO DO YOU HAVE TO APPROACH?

The first people you have to contact are those who will buy the articles, books or scripts which you produce as a result of your travels. They might be book publishers or magazine editors, travel editors on newspapers, or companies with interests in the part of the world you want to visit. These are the people who will pay for the time you are going to spend on the project.

The other group of people you need to contact are those who can supply you with flights, accommodation, drivers, guides, interpreters, background information and any other assistance you may need. These people could be government information officers, ministries of tourism, tour operators, conference bureaux, airlines, hoteliers, city tourist offices, international trade associations or local companies that export goods to your country. All these people have a vested interest in encouraging you to write favourably about their countries, their cities, their national products, their hotels, their resorts and their people. (See page 154.)

GETTING EDITORS TO FUND YOUR TRIPS

Some trade magazines manage to hire correspondents in other countries to report on the happenings of their industry worldwide, but not many. It is hard for them to find people who are able to write in English and who will be sufficiently motivated by the limited payments to supply copy regularly and on time.

Many of them, however, would like to carry more international news and features, since they can be useful to their readers — particularly if they talk about state-of-the-art practices which have not yet reached the magazine's home territory. They also help to establish the magazines as being international in their coverage.

In order to get this sort of international coverage some editors will be willing to fund at least part of your expenses themselves, and they may also have contacts from whom they can get cheap travel facilities.

Start by approaching every editor you have written for in the past, or who you think might be interested in using you in the future, and express your willingness to travel anywhere at any time on their behalf.

If an editor from a building magazine needs a story about, say, a new town being constructed in the South American jungle, he has several options. He could try to find someone over there to visit the site, write it up and send the copy back. But where would he find such a person? How could he be sure of the quality of the writing? How long would it take to arrive?

The next option is to go himself or send a staff writer. However the trip could take at least a week and might take more. He probably can't afford to be away that long on one story, and he almost certainly doesn't want to pay a staff writer a full week's expenses on top of their salary, just to have them away from the office for a week.

Supposing, therefore, he knows of a freelancer who would be willing to tackle the story for the usual fee, plus a free flight and hotel. If he knows and trusts that freelancer it looks like a good deal. Freelancers can afford to make offers like this to editors because they know they can cover other stories for other outlets while they are in that country.

GETTING GOVERNMENTS AND THE TRAVEL INDUSTRY TO FUND YOUR TRIPS

It is extraordinary how countries and cities will latch on to something which has been written about them in the past, and build a tourist industry around it. A country which has been used as the setting for a James Bond book or film, or has played host to Somerset Maugham, Noel Coward or Joseph Conrad, will use the fact wherever it can to promote its international image and bring in tourists and investment.

The fact that few writers can hope to give them this sort of immortality does not seem to matter. It is enough that you just keep reflecting the image they have established.

In every country you could ever want to visit, there will be at least one set of people who will have a vested interest in showing a writer their side of the story. The country's government might want to gain coverage in foreign media for some specific project they have undertaken – like the construction of a dam or the rebuilding of a city. Or they might want to stimulate trade or promote the products their country manufactures and exports. Whether they are selling cocoa beans or high technology, international publicity is something they need and want.

National tourist authorities want to reach potential tourists who can afford to travel to their country. A Caribbean island, for instance, will aim to attract certain sectors of the general public and the organisers of conference and incentive travel groups. It therefore wants to have travel articles written about how wonderful its beaches are, how luxurious its hotels, and so on.

Hotel owners want their establishments to be written about, as do the organisers of tours or special interest activities. Disney World wants to be written about just as much as Bangkok's Oriental Hotel or a company organising cricketing holidays in Corfu.

Freelancers can be particularly useful to all these people because they write for a variety of outlets, and because they will have to get their work published as widely as possible in order to earn a living and build up a reputation. Here the freelance writer has an advantage over the employed writer.

154

For instance, if a staff feature writer from a national paper wants to travel to Tahiti, the chance of getting an article into that paper might encourage the tourist authorities and other interested parties to agree to supply the flight, accommodation and whatever else is needed. If that journalist then writes a glowing article which encourages people to visit the island everyone will be happy. If, for whatever reason, the journalist doesn't enjoy the trip, can't find anything to write about, or the paper decides it doesn't have space for the piece, then the whole trip has been a waste of money. The journalist isn't too worried because he or she still draws a salary, and they have also had a free trip, but the Tahitian authorities have lost out.

By contrast, a successful freelancer might be able to place a dozen different articles about Tahiti in various magazines and papers. To achieve the same amount of coverage with staff journalists the Tahitians would have to pay out for twelve trips instead of one.

Organised Trips

As you become known to the tourism industry, they will begin to approach you with offers of hospitality. This is obviously easier than having to set everything up yourself but there are some drawbacks.

Most officially organised trips involve taking groups of journalists, with you as part of the group. This mean that there will be set itineraries. While they will do all they can to provide special facilities for individuals within the group who want to follow their own ideas, or they may arrange for you to stay on after the rest of the group has left, the amount of time you get to yourself will be limited.

Before accepting such offers, ask yourself how useful these organised trips will be. The answer will largely depend on who the other members of the group are. Do they have similar interests, and are you going to get on with them? And will the hosts be willing to adapt to your specific needs?

WHO ELSE CAN YOU SELL TO?

Having decided on your destination, you can then go to other media outside your core market, to ask if there is anything they would like covered while you are there.

For example a trip originally to cover the tourism and business travel industries in a particular foreign country would take on another dimension if another editor asked for a piece on national pastimes or the state of a particular national industry in that country.

One or two extra commissions like this at the outset of a project will make it a great deal easier to get funding from the authorities.

Foreign Editors

If you are going to write articles about international subjects, you should also be able to sell them to international outlets. For instance, if you are writing a travel piece for a magazine in your own country, the same piece could be of interest in numerous other countries. The only limitation is the language barrier, since translation costs are usually too high to be justifiable on anything but the most high-profile of stories.

Whenever you visit a country, try to meet the editors of relevant magazines based in that area. Not only are they a potential source of work for pieces from other destinations, they are also good sources of information on what is going on in their home markets.

The Specialist Press

Don't just concentrate on the prestige titles. Sometimes the smallest and most specialist magazines are the ones which are most in need of freelance contributions.

On one trip to Hong Kong, for instance, I was asked by a magazine serving the discotheque industry to interview the managements of the two or three best-known nightclubs in the islands, and by a cosmetics trade magazine to talk to the head of one of the giant cosmetic companies about the fashion for

Western-style make-up in the East, and what it means to the cosmetics industry. Both sets of research helped to broaden my understanding of life in the colony as a whole.

Book Publishers

Although articles are the bread and butter of the travel writer (with some radio and television talks as well if they are lucky), a book project can form the foundation of a trip. You might need to visit somewhere exotic in order to use it as a backdrop for a novel or film script, or to research part of a non-fiction subject. Perhaps you want to write a guidebook or cookery book; you might want to study the architecture of an area, or write up its history.

You will need to have a clear idea of the book's subject if you are going to interest a publisher. Just going to the Amazon Rainforest will not be enough to persuade them to pay you an advance and give you their stamp of approval. However if you already have a track record for writing about the environment and conservation, or if you have written other travel books in a similar style, or if they are producing a series of guidebooks and need one from the area you are visiting, then you could be in business.

Once you have been commissioned to write a book, you will have a stronger basis for approaching magazine editors, since they will be able to see more clearly the purpose of your visit, and will feel more confident that you are going to undertake some serious research.

You may find that the tourist authorities and other interested parties are more impressed by the short-term potential of articles than the long-term possibilities of a book. But the very fact that you are a commissioned author will add to your credibility.

WHO PAYS THE AIR FARE?

If you have to pay several hundreds (or even several thousands) for a ticket, the chances of making a profit from the trip are very slight indeed. You either need to persuade someone else (like an editor) to pay for you, or you need to talk an airline into giving you a free seat.

Some countries have a nationalised airline, or at least an airline which is closely affiliated to their tourist authorities. If you can convince those tourist authorities that you are worthy of a trip, they may well be able to get you a free air ticket. Similarly, if you offer a tour operator coverage of their products in the consumer or travel trade press, they may give you a ticket to the destinations where they operate.

Sometimes, however, you can start by securing the flight and can then build the rest of the trip around it. This means approaching the airlines cold and explaining why it would be advantageous to them to carry you for nothing. This can be difficult, since there are a limited number of outlets for articles about airlines and flights, mainly because all the major ones are so similar there is virtually nothing new you can say about them.

There might, however, be an opportunity to interview the airline's chief executive or other members of staff, or there might be a business story in which you can mention the airline as the major carrier to the area. Airlines can be mentioned in travel features if they supply the market with specialised services of any sort. You might also be able to contribute an article to an in-flight magazine, a travel trade paper or an airline trade magazine.

Getting the flight is the hardest part, and you may sometimes have to bite the bullet, especially at the beginning of your career, and pay for the flight yourself in order to get started. Only do this if you are sure that the trip will give you enough material to offset the costs; or if you feel the experience is worth investing your own money in, whether or not you can recoup your expenses through sales.

WHERE DO YOU START?

These are your first steps:

1 Decide on your destination and be certain that you are going to get there.

2   Find out as much as possible about it — reading books, approaching their embassy or consulate and tourism office, getting travel information.

3   Contact every editor or publisher who might conceivably be interested in commissioning work of any sort from the destination.

4   As well as contacting the tourist authorities for the country as a whole, find out which cities have their own promotional organisations. Contact international trade organisations, tour operators, airlines, hoteliers and anyone else you can think of. Tell them that you are going to be visiting their country/city/island, and tell them which magazines or book publishers have agreed to buy or look at the resulting work, and which ones you have written for in the past (enclose copies of your previously published work). Ask if they can give you any help with information and travel facilities.

5   Once the trip is finalised, see which other places you could visit while you are there. When I took a flight to New Zealand, for instance, I discovered that the plane also stopped in Hawaii, Tahiti and Fiji. I was therefore able to contact all the relevant authorities in these islands, tell them that I was going to be flying in, and ask if they could make arrangements for me to stay a few days and see various things. Turning one destination into several, with the investment of just a few more days of your time, can make the difference between profit or loss on a trip. Similarly, however, staying a week too long, following up stories which don't work, can also undermine the financial viability of a trip. It is a balancing act.

6   Approach any of your own country's international companies who might be active in the area, and ask if they would like any research done. They might, for instance, want something about their local branch for their head office magazine, or to send to a trade paper, or they might

simply give you the name of someone out there who will help you with introductions.

BACKGROUND READING

The broader your background research, the more intelligently you will be able to write about a place, because you will have a better idea of where to look for the angles and what questions to ask once you get there. This doesn't just mean reading dry history and geography books. Novels can be just as useful – and sometimes more so – in giving colour and life to a place both before you visit and while you are there.

The books don't have to be current, and they don't have to be particularly literary or learned. They just have to give you another insight into the place, stimulate your interest and imagination, and feed you ideas and perspectives which will help in your research.

When you reach your destination, make a point of asking about books which are good for giving local colour, and browse through any bookstalls you pass. There may be some classics of local literature which have never been published internationally but which will be packed with helpful detail and will inspire you to sample different aspects of the local life for yourself.

WHEN YOU GET THERE

Do As Much As Possible

However comfortable it may seem, you must resist the temptation to spend your time just sitting on the beach, or being led docilely around by the tourist authorities to view endless hotel bedrooms and conference banqueting suites. You may have to do some of this sort of research for your projects, but as soon as you feel you have got enough material, explain that you now want to do something else. The clearer you are in your mind about what you want to see and who you want to talk to, the easier it will be for your hosts to arrange it for you, or at least suggest how you can arrange it yourself, if you have not already done so.

If there are one or two major stories you know you want to follow up, do as much of the preparation as possible before you leave home. Write to the people you want to interview, explaining who you are and why you want to talk to them. If you leave it until you get there you may find that they are unavailable and you don't want to waste valuable time while you are there on administrative tasks.

Get as wide a variety of experiences as possible. A trip to Bangkok, for instance, should include visits to the royal palaces as well as an investigation of the rural poverty which forces so many young Thais to sell their bodies in brothels and massage parlours. You want to understand what they eat and how they worship, what their homes are like and how they earn a living. You want to see their scenery and hear about their social problems.

However much you do, of course, you will only ever be able to scratch the surface of another culture by making a short visit. But the more scratches you can make during your stay, the more you are going to have to write about when you get home.

Search Out the Angles

You have to search out angles for stories in order to put together enough saleable material to make the trip pay for itself.

Search out the most interesting characters for an international readership. Should you interview the President, or someone running a revolutionary party? Or a nun doing charity work in the slums? Or an English family running a hotel in the African bush? Try to find ordinary people doing interesting jobs. A women's magazine might be interested in a policewoman working in the Hong Kong Vice Squad; a gay magazine might like a piece on a gay couple running a transvestite bar in Tahiti; a surfing magazine might like some background on people running beach businesses in Hawaii; and a golfing magazine is likely to want to know about golf courses everywhere, and will welcome comment from local professionals and club managers.

Don't try to write while you are on the trip − it's a waste of valuable time and you will lack a sense of perspective. If you find you have a spare day, go and seek out another story.

Keep every bit of background material you can lay your hands on, along with tapes, diaries, notebooks and whatever else you use to record your experiences. There will be plenty of time to sort it all out when you get back home.

WHEN YOU GET BACK

Once you have written the articles which were specifically commissioned before you left, you can then look at what else you have managed to come back with.

List all the possible stories you think you have enough material to substantiate, and for each one, give a list of possible angles and outlets. For instance, if you have toured around Israel, visiting all the main centres of interest, you might be able to break the trip down into a number of different pieces:

- Visiting Jerusalem
- Visiting Tel Aviv
- Visiting Bethlehem
- Floating in the Dead Sea
- Staying on a Kibbutz
- Holidaying in a War Zone
- Making the Desert Bloom

You can then look at ways in which each of these subjects can be adapted to suit different outlets. A piece on the therapeutic powers of the Dead Sea, for instance, might suit a health and medical magazine as well as the travel pages of a national paper. It could also be included in a general round-up of the whole tour for another magazine. A magazine for the hotel industry might be interested to know how the hotels on the Dead Sea attract people to the lowest point on earth and create travel packages based on the health-giving properties of the water.

A piece on staying in a kibbutz could be of interest to a

162

national paper or magazine as well as to a publication aimed at students and younger travellers. It might also be of interest to a farming or horticultural magazine, linking in to the 'Making the Desert Bloom' idea. If you spend some time thinking about the different permutations you will be surprised by how many there are.

Writing Up the Articles

Because you have been given so much for nothing by your hosts, you may feel obliged to write favourably about everything you have seen and heard. They certainly hope you will, and they will have shown you aspects of their countries which they hope you and your future readers will like and enjoy. That does not mean, however, that you should be afraid to be truthful in what you write.

Your only duty is to write honestly and interestingly about everything you have seen. If you have been commissioned to write a piece about the conference facilities on a particular Caribbean island and they turn out to be non-existent, then you have to say so. However there's no reason why you shouldn't write another piece for a brides' magazine about the suitability of the island as a honeymoon destination because of the intimacy of the hotels and the peaceful atmosphere.

There are always a number of facets to any place, and because you choose to write a piece about the scandal of child labour in the factories of Thailand for one magazine, it does not mean that you can't write another article praising the scenic beauties of the country for tourists, or the wonders of their national cuisine for gourmets.

Bear in mind that if you get a reputation solely as a muck-raking journalist you will find it increasingly difficult to get people to help finance your trips. However if you succeed in finding and selling exposé stories, you should either be able to get editors to pay your expenses as you become more established, or raise your prices to cover the costs yourself.

THE COSTS AND BENEFITS

The problem with travel writing is that it is very time-consuming. So you have to be sure that the resulting books and articles are going to earn enough money to cover the time you spend 'on the road' as well as the time you spend 'at the word-processor'. In order to get the figures to balance, you need to squeeze every last ounce of material out of every trip.

Against this, however, you can set the enormous value of the experiences you are having, and the enormous boost to your professional credibility. If you can show a potential customer a collection of published work which is the result of your own globe-trotting efforts, they are going to see at a glance that you are highly motivated, well-organised and professional. A reputation like that is beyond price.

16

Ghostwriting

Some people find it hard to understand why anyone would want to be a ghostwriter. 'Don't you find it frustrating.' they enquire, 'to do all that work and let someone else take the glory?'

The glib answer is 'No, because I still get the money,' but that is by no means the whole story.

Other people question the ethics of the authors who pass material off as being their own when they have in fact employed a ghost to write it for them. Those same people, however, probably wouldn't be worried by the idea that the President of the United States or the British Prime Minister do not have time to write their own speeches. Not many people outside the political arena could name a single speech-writer. Yet most would still agree that speech-writing is an interesting job to have − and a perfectly ethical practice.

The actual content of a ghosted book nearly always comes from the mind of the named author; it is simply shaped and presented by the ghost. It's like hiring someone to redecorate your house. You can still make all the important decisions, telling the interior designer what sort of effects you want to achieve and taking their advice along the way. But then you will probably leave them to get on with the job. It is still your house and the taste and ideas will still largely be yours. You have merely employed an expert to execute your ideas.

WHY BECOME A GHOSTWRITER?

The Money

The first reason to take ghostwriting assignments is the money. Whether you are writing articles for businesspeople to send to their trade papers, or autobiographies for Hollywood film stars, it is nearly always better paid than creating the same material in your own name would be.

Take the case of the businessman wanting to get into a trade paper. He has a vested interest in being published and will be willing to pay someone who can help him achieve this without having to spend agonising hours staring at a blank sheet of paper. A businessman is used to paying for the professional advice of lawyers, accountants, advertising people and photographers, so a writer's daily rate is unlikely to frighten him off. (Apart from anything else, he can compare it to his own earnings and see that it is not unreasonable.)

In the case of the Hollywood film star, controversial athlete, pop singer, politician or notorious criminal, the publishers can afford to pay larger advances because they know that the star's name will guarantee a certain number of sales of the book, particularly if they are willing to be personally involved in the promotion of the story with appearances on chat shows and interviews with the press. In some cases the publisher will be able to recoup almost all of the advance payment by selling parts of the story to a national newspaper for serialisation. If the author has international appeal they can earn massive amounts from similar deals all round the world.

Most people who are in a position to require a ghostwriter can almost certainly command larger fees for their words than the people who do the ghosting for them. They will probably be able to sell more books as well. There is consequently going to be more money in the pot which the ghost can earn a share of.

The Experience

Anyone who is going to make a full-time living as a freelance writer needs to collect as much high-grade information as possible, because that is their stock in trade.

Ghosting a book for someone is like being paid to be educated by the best teachers in the world. Imagine, for instance, being asked to ghost *The Origin of the Species* for Darwin, or *The Decline and Fall of the Roman Empire* for Gibbon. Imagine being paid to learn everything that is in the heads of these people and then turning their thoughts, words and notes into book form. Could there be a better form of education?

Of course, not all the people who use ghostwriters are going to create books of such lasting value. But suppose one of your specialist areas is information technology. If you get invited to ghost for one of the most famous experts on the subject you will be able to ask questions about the future, and learn things at his knee, which other people would have to pay good money for, in the form of consultancy or seminar fees.

The Contacts

Not only does a ghost meet the greatest experts in his or her various fields of interest, they are also able to meet and work with the publishers in the same field.

Occasionally a ghostwriter will be hired by the author, and even the publisher will never know about their involvement, but more often it is the publisher who instigates the relationship, and it provides excellent opportunities to build a long-term working partnership. Frequently the authors of the books are busy people and hard to get hold of. Sometimes they are temperamental in some way. The publishers consequently rely on ghosts to act as go-betweens and to make the process of publication as smooth as possible. This enables the ghosts to demonstrate their skill, tact and diplomacy, thus increasing the chances of securing further work from the same publisher.

The Chance to Produce More Books

By ghosting books for other people, and hiding behind their names, a writer is able to produce far more books than the market could bear if they were all appearing under his or her own name. It is quite possible to write a book of 70,000 words in two months if the material is immediately available, whereas you could never achieve such a fast turnround if you had to do all the research from scratch.

The trade would find it hard to believe that any author could produce up to six books a year and hope to find readers for all of them. By having most, or all, of that output coming out under other people's names, the credibility problem is removed. No publisher, bookseller or reader need ever know quite how prolific you are. And a few ghosting projects each year could increase your earning potential considerably.

WHERE DOES THE WORK COME FROM?

When it comes to books, celebrities are usually approached by publishers rather than the other way round. While they are usually flattered to be asked, they often don't have time to do the writing themselves, or they do not think they will be able to do it well enough. The publisher will then offer to find a ghost.

With articles, the impetus generally comes from the public relations industry, which wants to get its clients' names into the media but can't get them to sit down and write the pieces themselves. These same people could also be potential authors of books.

The ghost can sell his or her services to either publishers or authors, and can sometimes be the prime mover in bringing the two together in the first place, acting like a talent scout for the publisher and an agent for the author. As in any business, the person who gets out and makes projects happen is always going to be more successful than the one who sits by the phone waiting for someone to call.

The Publishers

It is up to writers to tell publishers if they are interested in doing ghosting work. You need to ensure that the moment a publisher has a need for a ghost, your name comes to mind and your telephone number comes to hand.

From the publishers'point of view, the most important thing is that you should be known to be reliable and efficient, and that you are unlikely to fall out with the author or cause trouble at a later stage over credits. Any author who wants to get regular ghosting assignments needs to build relationships of trust with as many publishers as possible. Once you have turned in one or two books on time and without complications, they will always think of you first when the need arises.

The need might be a sudden demand for a topical book about someone who is in the news but who can't write it themselves, or it might arise when a commissioned book has either not arrived or has arrived in such a poor state that it needs to be completely rewritten. In either case there is likely to be some urgency about the project. The publisher may already have advertised the book to the trade as coming out in a few months' time and he can't afford to be let down.

The problem for the would-be ghostwriter is how to get a publisher to give you that first assignment. These are the steps to take:

1   Write them letters, just as you would when introducing yourself to a magazine editor. Explain what you have done in the past (mention any books you have had published already), and list your specialist areas. It is always easier for people to call your name to mind if they can associate you with a particular sort of work. Also, it is hard to believe that a writer can cover all subjects equally well. Tell publishers who specialise in showbusiness subjects about your experience in that area, tell publishers of travel books about your international experience, publishers of management books about your business writing activities and so on.

2   Send them any leaflets or brochures you have had printed, to explain what you have done in the past and what sort of work you would like to be considered for.

3   Send them copies of any published books you have written, with an explanatory note on why you think the skills you have shown in authoring this book would qualify you for ghosting projects. However, sending out books is expensive, so you will need to target this sort of mailing very carefully, only sending copies to publishers that you are sure use ghosts and who specialise in your areas of expertise.

4   Some people find it difficult to make telephone enquiries but they are a useful preliminary to an expensive mailing of books. You just have to ask if they are ever likely to use ghostwriters, and whether they would be interested in seeing some of your published work. Keep detailed notes of their responses, even if they are negative, so that you can follow up with a letter at a later stage if you have a different proposition to put to them.

5   Advertising in the publishing trade press can also work, although it is hard to estimate how much to spend in the hope of being in the right issue at the right time.

6   Having said that ghosts must never fall out with the authors they are supposed to be serving, and even less with the publishers, it does help if your name can appear somewhere on the cover of the books you are most proud to be associated with. You may get billed as 'co-author', but more likely it will say 'by Big Shot, with Joe Bloggs', or 'as told to Joe Bloggs'. While it isn't worth turning down a job just because you aren't going to get a credit, it is worth asking for one, because other publishers will notice it. However you can never expect your credit to upstage the author's and, as we have seen, it wouldn't be to your advantage for your name to be too noticeable on too many books.

The Authors

Many experts and celebrities have it in the backs of their minds that they would like to write books one day, either autobiographies or how-to books on their professional subjects, or something on one of their hobbies. For instance, a well-known actress might want to write about gardening or cooking, but won't know where to start.

These authors may need help with the actual writing or with finding a publisher. If they have already found a publisher (or have been approached by one), then they probably can't see how they can justify the time it will take them to produce a manuscript against the money the publishers are offering.

Only in exceptional cases is the money a publisher offers as an advance enough to make a difference to a celebrity. For many of these people there is more of a public relations benefit in having a book published than a financial one. A film star's biography will help to sell whatever film they are in at the moment, and will also remind producers and backers in Hollywood that the star is alive, well and bankable. For a businessperson, a book can enhance their credibility and that of their company.

If someone in this position is approached by a ghost who is willing to do all the work, they will probably be less interested in the money than in the speed and ease with which the book can be written. If the ghost can convince them that it will only take up a few days of their time to talk through the ideas and stories for the book, they may agree to sign over half the money the book earns, or offer the ghost a generous fee upfront. or a cut of the royalties if the book is likely to be a best-seller. In many cases they are happy to let the publisher sort out the financial details for them.

Many other people who are not famous, certainly not outside their own professional peer groups, still have useful books in them. They could be people who have had a particular adventure or harrowing experience, or people with a new diet to promote, or some sort of training skill.

In these cases the ghosts can work almost like agents. They can listen to whatever the prospective author has to talk about, prepare a synopsis for them, and perhaps write a specimen chapter. They can then submit the package to likely publishers on the author's behalf, or leave the author to do the submitting, remaining invisibly in the background, ready to write the rest of the book when a publisher takes the bait.

Many businesspeople decide to write books as promotional tools for themselves and their work. They may not be famous to start with, but they hope that authoring the book will help them become better known, giving them a public platform from which to promote themselves. In these cases they have a vested interest in getting the book published. They may even agree to buy a certain number of copies of the final book, which will help to persuade a publisher that it is a viable proposition. (For further details on vanity publishing, see Chapter 18.)

In such cases, the author may be willing to commission the ghost to produce the synopsis and specimen chapter, and may also agree to pay a 'success fee' when a reputable publisher agrees to take the book on. However in the case of books by individuals about their experiences, the ghost cannot usually expect to get money for this side of the service. He or she will then have to weigh up the chances of getting an offer from a publisher, and whether or not the book is likely to become a big seller, before agreeing to a share of the earnings rather than a fee.

It is always wise to involve a publisher early on. So many manuscripts are rejected by publishers every year that it would be very unwise for an author to commission a ghost to write a complete book on spec. Likewise, a ghost would be very unwise to agree to write a whole book on the offchance that it will sell at the end.

If, for whatever reason, an author asks you to produce a completed manuscript which will then be sold to a publisher, insist on being paid in advance and do not enter into any royalties deals unless they are in addition to the initial fee. The odds against success are too high, and the money in the bank is always better than the promise of some mythical future pay-off.

With an average-selling book there won't be enough money involved to make it a financially worthwhile project for an

172

author and a ghost. But if there is a likelihood of reprints, paperback editions, foreign rights sales or film rights, then it might be worth your while agreeing not to charge anything at the beginning in exchange for an agreed share of the profits (probably 50/50 for an unknown author, perhaps less for you if the author is well-known and has a stronger negotiating hand).

If you are in any doubt about the likely success of a project, make sure you get a fee in advance which is high enough to make the project worthwhile, even if you never get another penny from royalties.

GHOSTWRITING ARTICLES

Ghosting articles is part of the business writer's function. A company managing director may be advised by his public relations consultant to write articles which can be published in the relevant media as part of a more extensive campaign. The same person may, if well known, also be approached by the editors themselves and asked to write for special features or on specific topics.

Bylined articles are an excellent way of putting forward a company line, since the author is expected to be partisan and is therefore given far more leeway than a professional writer would be to blow the company trumpet and state its point of view.

However not many managing directors have the time to write articles (just as they don't have time to write their own speeches). If they can talk their thoughts through for an hour with a ghost, secure in the knowledge that they will see a draft of the article before it goes out in their name, they will normally be greatly relieved.

When they see the writer's draft they may well throw their hands up in horror and say that it is all wrong, but they will find it a great deal easier to correct and embellish what has already been committed to paper than to create the whole article from scratch. (Normally people in this situation throw up their hands in horror to start with, but when they actually sit down to make the changes they end up doing little more than tweaking and polishing.)

LINKING ARTICLES WITH BOOKS

There can also be a link between articles and books, since someone who has enough information for a number of articles may also be persuaded to put their name to a book, and someone who has authored a book will usually be interested in promoting it with articles. A ghost who is already familiar with the subject after writing a book is going to be a natural choice for writing the articles, and vice versa.

If you are receiving royalties for the book it will be in your interest to market and promote it in any way possible, and getting articles into the media is one of the most effective methods of selling books. It may also be possible to write some of the articles used to promote the book under your own name, giving a more objective view of the author and the content. These intricate relationships are only possible, however, if there is a strong bond of mutual trust between the author, the ghost, the publisher and any magazine or newspaper editors involved.

If it is obvious that your role as a ghost will prejudice your journalistic judgement regarding the subject, then you should explain your situation to editors at the beginning. It may make one or two of them discount you as a reliable source, but others will see it as confirmation that you know your material in depth.

17

Agents –
Who Needs Them?

WHAT DO AGENTS DO?

An agent is someone who will sell your work for you, and look after all the financial and legal details. They will check the terms of the contracts and ensure that you get the best possible deals. For this service they take a percentage of everything they sell for you (usually ten per cent, sometimes fifteen per cent), but they make no other charges apart, possibly, from asking you to pay expenses like postage and photocopying once a book has been sold.

They are only really interested in people who are writing books, films or plays, simply because there isn't enough money in writing articles or short stories to make it worth their while. Editors of most newspapers and magazines would be very surprised to be approached by a writer's agent rather than directly by a writer, unless it was a really major name. And agents wouldn't know anything about selling business writing services.

When writers are starting out, it is comforting for them to believe that if they could just be discovered by an agent all their problems would be over. They would be able to retreat back into their shells and let these ruthless businesspeople take care of everything. Once in a while that might happen, but don't hold your breath waiting!

Agents act as filters for publishers, and for the writers they can provide selling, negotiating and legal services. Many of them are less adept at some of these things than the writers they represent, but because the writers want to concentrate on other things and not be bothered with the details of contracts and sub-clauses, even bad agents are able to get the business.

Agents will seldom 'build a career' for anyone, or shape them in any way at all. But that doesn't mean they can't help writers increase their income and broaden their scope. Some of them are very helpful indeed, and can improve a writer's financial situation considerably by getting better deals and arranging subsidiary rights sales. But the initial impetus on any project must always come from the writer. You are the creator of the product, the instigator of the ideas. Agents cannot do that for you, but they *can* help you decide how to market your products and reap the maximum benefit.

Good agents are in great demand, and can pick and choose the authors they take on. They are also very low-profile, and the only way a writer is likely to find out about them is by questioning other writers or looking them up in one of the general writers' guides listed in the Bibliography.

WHAT DO PUBLISHERS THINK OF THEM?

Most publishers will have one or two agents whom they respect and enjoy doing business with. They will be the ones who have brought them books which have done well in the past, and who they feel have dealt with them fairly and efficiently. When asked to comment on agents in general, however, their noses tend to wrinkle up.

Most will admit that they receive as many badly presented and unsuitable manuscripts from people who call themselves agents as they get direct from writers. They will grudgingly admit that agents can sometimes get larger advances from them than the writers themselves might achieve.

Yet, despite the fact that they tend to be sniffy about the agenting profession in general, publishers continue to recommend that writers go to agents first, rather than sending manuscripts directly to them. This is because they hope that at least some of the flood of bad material will be stemmed by agents who will either discourage the writers from continuing or will help put the manuscripts or ideas into a saleable form.

DO YOU NEED AN AGENT?

If you are brimming with ideas on how to market your own material, you may do better without an agent at the beginning of your career, but it doesn't hurt to start putting out feelers to see if there is someone out there who will be enthusiastic about what you have to offer and will help you to progress.

If you are lucky you might find an agent who is really capable of showing you the shortcomings of your work and advising you on how to improve it and make it saleable. Even if they just listen to your ideas and tell you which ones are unlikely to work, they are saving you the time you might have wasted developing fruitless projects.

You must, however, find someone who you genuinely believe is giving you useful advice, and not merely criticising or praising your work for ulterior motives. If that is the case then you will simply be wasting time which could be better spent learning how to market your work yourself.

Agents can only sell what you give them. They will seldom get commissions for you from editors, or ghostwriting jobs, or any of the other assignments writers need to stay in business. Every so often, a commission or ghostwriting job will fall into an agent's lap, but that is pure luck.

Some established authors don't bother with agents. They simply hire solicitors to sort out the legal side of their relationships with publishers, preferring to keep the marketing of their work to themselves. A good agent should be able to act like a solicitor.

The problem for agents is that they generally only charge a ten or fifteen per cent commission on anything they sell for you. That means that if they get you a £3,000 advance on a book (which is not unusually low for an unknown writer), they are only making between £300 and £450. For it to be worth their while, they need to believe that you have a glittering future ahead of you, with a steady flow of royalties which they can take a percentage of.

In order to keep their businesses going, they have to concentrate their efforts on their established and high-earning protegés, people they know they can rely on to create turnover for their companies. That doesn't mean they never take on new writers, or writers in lower income brackets, but it does mean that they can only devote a limited amount of their time to each, nothing like the time you can devote to your own business affairs.

HOW DO YOU FIND A GOOD AGENT?

Trying to find an agent can be as soul-destroying as trying to find a publisher. The process is very similar, with the same likelihood of rejection. What makes this stage of the hunt even more depressing, however, is knowing that even if you succeed in finding an agent, you may still fail to find a publisher.

On the positive side, however, an agent who agrees to read and comment on your work will be providing you with objective and, ideally, professional advice.

Like publishers, agents work very slowly indeed. You can send in a manuscript and then hear nothing for months, finally receiving a printed rejection slip every bit as impersonal as anything a publisher might send you.

So, somewhere out there may be an agent who is perfect for you; someone who will appreciate your potential and will be able to give you objective criticism of your work and help you sell it. But while you are finding them, and then listening to their criticism, acting on it and waiting for them to do anything for you, you are going to starve to death.

What Should You Send an Agent?

Start by selling your own products, but every so often float one of them around the agents listed in one of the general writers' guides (see Bibliography). The best projects to send them are the ones which are likely to be complicated legally or which have the potential to sell into a number of different markets. If, for instance, you have a book which you believe is a potential best-seller, and you think it could well go into paperback, sell to America and make the basis for a film or television series, then an agent will be able to coordinate all those various strands of the operation for you.

If, on the other hand, you think your idea will make a straightforward book, and you can get it accepted by a reputable publisher on your own, you will be offered a standard contract with standard terms. In this case, there is little point in giving ten per cent of your payment to an agent, since there will be little they can do to improve on the deal you can get for yourself, and they might even succeed in messing up a good relationship by being too aggressive with the publisher in order to justify their existence.

How Do You Sell Yourself to an Agent?

You have to sell yourself and your ideas to agents in just the same way as you do to potential customers. That means not inundating them with massive manuscripts unless they have agreed to read them. Always start with a letter which sums up in a few paragraphs what a book or script is about. If you are selling fiction then include a few sample pages from the beginning of the book — no more!

There is no reason why you shouldn't send the same package to several agents at once, provided you personalise the letters so that they don't realise. They will squawk indignantly if they find out that you have done this, but at this stage you need to talk to as many of them as possible as quickly as possible.

BUILDING A RELATIONSHIP WITH AN AGENT

Once you have found an agent you like — and liking them is probably the most important reason for choosing someone at the beginning — you will then have to make a commitment to them, and agree not to be represented by anyone else. If things don't work out you can always change your agent later.

179

Just because you have asked an agent to represent you in the selling of a particular project, however, there is no reason why you can't go on selling the rest of your work yourself. The good ones won't insist that you give them everything you do anyway. They will hope to establish a relationship of mutual trust so that over the years you gradually come to rely on them more and more.

Until that relationship has been achieved however, and until you can see that the money is flowing in satisfactorily, you would be mad to trust your entire livelihood to the hands of another person. Whatever promises they might make, and however rosy a picture they paint of your future with them, you should keep control of your own destiny to start with. The bulk of your income must come from your own marketing efforts, with anything the agent earns being treated as extra. When the agent is earning more for you than you can earn for yourself, you can hand the whole business over and concentrate on writing.

If an agent wants you to sign a contract with them, you should think very carefully about it. You need to find someone you can trust, and they need to trust you − so why do they want you to sign anything? If you feel certain that you want to work with them and they still insist on you signing a contract, then get a solicitor to glance at it first.

Personally I don't think that someone at the beginning of their career should be asked to sign anything. As you become more established, and your financial affairs become more complex, that situation might change, and it might become more important to you to have the agent who drives the hardest deals rather than one you completely trust or even like.

Some agencies charge a reading fee to try to recoup some income from the hours and days they spend looking at submissions from writers. Unless you have been recommended to try that particular agency by someone whose judgement you trust, I would advise never paying anything. Most of the good agents do not make any charge.

On balance, a good agent can help a writer a great deal, and a bad agent can slow their progress down. You do not need to have an agent to succeed, but any friend and ally you can make in your battle for survival should be treasured.

18

Vanity Publishing

The golden rule is that writers should never pay publishers to publish their work for them ... unless they are completely clear about what they are buying for their money, and know exactly how they will sell the resulting books.

Vanity publishers are the companies which advertise for authors, poets and writers in the press (usually the classified ads of the nationals and similar publications). The advertisements are designed to appeal to the many thousands of people who have written books and had them rejected by the established publishing companies.

Certain that the publishers are mistaken in their judgements, these would-be authors decide to prove the world wrong by putting their own money into the production of the book, and the vanity publishers are waiting in the wings to do the work for them.

When you send your work to a vanity publisher they will praise it and make a great many promises about how well they believe it will sell. They will claim to undertake all the functions of an ordinary publisher, and will promise to pay royalties on sales. They will ask, however, that you pay them a fee for this service in advance, which will be a great deal higher than any normal printer would charge.

Once they have your money they may print and bind a certain number of copies of your book – perhaps to a reasonable standard and perhaps not. They may leave these books in a warehouse or they may deliver them to your home. What they will not do is get your book into the bookshops at the same level as the established publishers. They may get it into one or two shops, they may even sell a few copies, but more often they won't.

The least scrupulous ones may not even carry out the production work they have promised to do. The better ones will do a good job of the production, and may even advertise a few of the best books they create to the trade (asking you to contribute to the advertising costs), but they will still not be able to fulfil the expectations of most aspiring authors.

The morality of what they are doing is irrelevant. In every walk of life there are people selling products which promise more than they can possibly deliver, from cosmetics advertised by models who would be beautiful whatever they put on their faces to DIY products which purport to be easy to assemble (and are in fact quite the opposite for many of the unskilled people they are sold to). Vanity publishers are offering a service and it is up to you to decide whether you think it is one which will help you in any way or merely cause you disappointment and expense.

WHEN MIGHT VANITY PUBLISHING BE WORTHWHILE?

In some cases, it might be reasonable to make a financial contribution towards the publication of your book, provided the company you are dealing with provides a professional service.

For instance, perhaps you want to write a book of memoirs about your old army regiment, and you know that there are several thousand ex-soldiers from the same regiment who would be happy to buy a copy at a price which will easily cover the cost of production and distribution.

Alternatively, you might be running a village farm shop, and

182

feel sure you can sell your customers a book of healthy recipes using natural products. You are willing to invest some money in producing such a book for its promotional value, knowing you will be able to cover your costs with the cover price, or with increased sales of certain products in your shop.

Perhaps you run a training course, and you want to be able to give each delegate a copy of a book written by you on the subjects covered in the course. You have worked out that you will be able to write off the cost of publishing the book by including it in the price of the course.

There are a number of such situations in which you might be able to justify paying for the publication of a book. But in all these cases it would be better to approach a reputable publisher and come to an arrangement with them, rather than simply pay money to a vanity publisher who has no track record for producing quality books, and who can offer no hope of you earning back any of your money.

Let's take the farm shop as an example and follow it through. You could start by offering the idea in the normal way to a number of relevant publishers. After all, the book would carry even more weight with your customers if it was on sale in bookshops as well as in your shop, and if they saw it reviewed in magazines and heard you interviewed on local radio.

If none of the publishers can see a wide enough market for the book to justify buying it, you can then write back to them explaining that if the book was published you would be willing to buy a certain number of copies from them, and asking if that would make them change their minds.

It may be that they thought your book was up to publishable standards, but doubted that they would be able to sell enough copies to make it financially worthwhile. If you are offering to buy a thousand or more copies, that will change their calculations completely. Their costs will be covered and any copies they are able to sell through the normal channels will be pure profit for them.

Look at what you get by doing it this way:

- The editorial judgement and skills of a top publisher, who will be able to advise you on how to improve the book, and will edit it to the highest professional standards.

- The design skills of a top publisher to produce a cover which will look completely professional, and to oversee any illustrations.
- A distribution network which is already established and respected by the book trade, and a publicity department which will help you get the book reviewed and written about.
- A well-known publisher's imprint on the book which is recognised as bona fide by all who know about such things, and which endorses the content of the book.
- An opportunity for you to take a professionally created product – the book – and promote it in any way you choose, and as a consequence promote your own business at the same time.
- A chance to receive royalty payments if the book is successful in the general market.

HOW CAN PROFESSIONAL WRITERS HELP?

As described in Chapter 16 on ghostwriting, a professional writer can go to the owner of the farm shop, or the training course organiser, or the old soldier, and can offer to help both with the writing and with setting up the publishing deal. This is another way writers can generate work for themselves, getting fees from the 'author' or the publisher or both, depending on each individual situation.

The freelance writer can also help to promote the book with articles about, and interviews with, the author, or can ghost them in his or her name, being paid either by the media that print them or the author.

Be warned: there are unscrupulous people around who claim to help people write books for publication when they actually stand no chance of succeeding. The only way to ensure that you, as a writer, do not get classed with these people is to deal exclusively with established publishing houses who can market the resulting books properly. Also, you should only ask for payment from the 'author' when you have succeeded in finding a publisher who will take the book on.

BOOKS THAT PUBLISHERS WON'T BE INTERESTED IN

Some books are so personal in their interest — like histories of one particular family, or biographies of people who are only known to their friends and relatives, or novels which have no general appeal — that the major publishers will not be willing to put their imprint on them, even if the writer offers to buy copies. No reputable publisher wants books which will damage their professional standing to appear under their name. They certainly don't want to become known as vanity publishers.

If you are determined to go ahead with publishing such a book, and you are fully aware that you are not going to see any financial return, then you can begin to look for publishers who will be willing to do the editing, designing and printing work for you, even if they are not willing to put their name on the book, or include it in their lists or catalogues.

It would still be better to find a publisher whose books you have seen and liked in the bookshops, who will be willing to help you out (for a fee, of course), than to go to one who is advertising for authors and makes his living solely from the money paid by the writers.

If you can't persuade any reputable publisher to help you, and you still want to go ahead (which you probably shouldn't, since it is unlikely that they are all wrong), then approach several of the people who advertise, and compare the contracts they offer and samples of previous books they have done. If possible, visit them in person to see if you like and trust them before committing yourself to anything.

Be warned: I have never heard of anyone making money from a book produced by a vanity publisher, so don't be fooled by any false promises, and expect to lose your money.

19

Becoming
Your Own Publisher

You don't always have to rely on other people to get your work produced and distributed. You may decide to take on the role of the publisher yourself, and reap the benefits. However you have to face the fact that you will also reap the extra work and take the risk of losing your money.

It's like a skilled furniture-maker deciding how to reach his customers. He could sell his furniture to shops and department stores. He knows they will put a 100 per cent mark-up on everything they buy from him, but he also knows they will take away all the worry of marketing and selling the goods, leaving him free to get on with creating the next bit of furniture.

Alternatively, he could open a small shop himself, or advertise his goods and get people to come to the workshop to buy or commission direct. That way he cuts out the middleman and takes all the profit himself. He only has to make half as much furniture in order to turn over the same amount of money, but he has to invest money in advertising and property, and time into talking to customers and doing administrative work.

Many of the same choices face the writer. It is quite possible, if you choose to do so, to use your writing skills to build a full-sized business, perhaps ending up with a large staff of employees. But is that what you really want?

BOOKS

If you have an idea for a book, and you believe you can market it as well as, or better than, an established publisher, then it could be more profitable for you to publish it yourself than to take the royalties offered in an author-only deal.

Self-publishing is unlikely to work with something like a novel, because a broad, general readership is hard to target cost-effectively and therefore requires the backing of a publisher. However if you write about gardening, DIY, finance, law or any other specialist subject, then you will be able to promote your book to target groups in a number of ways:

- You could advertise in the relevant special interest magazines.
- You could send direct mail items to lists of potential buyers through book clubs, associations and institutes.
- You could sell the book through retailers specialising in your product area, such as DIY shops for a book on plumbing, or record shops for a book on reggae music, rather than traditional, all-purpose bookshops which seldom manage to attract pop music fans or DIY enthusiasts.

Putting a Book Together

Many different skills are involved in creating a book, apart from the writing. If you can do all the editorial, design, production and marketing work yourself, you will be at a great advantage. However most people need help with at least one or other of these aspects, and you will find details of several freelance editors, designers and publicity consultants in the books listed in the Bibliography under 'General Writers' Guides'. Printers and typesetters are best found through directories, recommendations, or just looking at the printing details listed at the front of any book you particularly like the look of. Publishing a book is often quite a complex and expensive business so you would be wise to consult the books listed in the Bibliography under 'Self-Publishing'.

Selling Your Book

While it is very nice to see your book in the windows of high street bookshops, and even nicer to have the general public going in and asking for your work by name, the logistics of marketing to bookshops are highly uneconomic for most self-publishers.

Only a few of the major chains have any sort of central buying process. The rest buy individually, which means that you could spend a whole morning visiting a bookshop which only agrees to buy one or two copies of the book. Also, many booksellers are unwilling to see anyone other than sales reps from large publishers or wholesalers.

If you feel that bookshops are likely to be a major source of sales for your book, you will almost certainly have to set up a mail-order operation rather than slogging round to them in person. And you will need to ensure that they can locate and order the book should someone come in asking for it.

You will need to apply for an International Standard Book Number (ISBN). This number helps educational authorities, computer-using distributors, and booksellers using tele-ordering systems to locate and order your book when required. It also means that you will be paid a fee by public libraries when your book is lent out. In addition you need to get your title included in any relevant lists of books in print (see Useful Addresses).

Your main aim should be to locate customers who have the potential to buy large numbers of books at one time. Interested companies might be able to use them as promotional gifts. (For instance, a travel company might buy a travel guide to give to customers, a motoring organisation might buy a car maintenance handbook and so on.) It's also well worth approaching specialised clubs or associations which have an efficient means of selling to their members like catalogues or direct marketing campaigns. These are all markets which can be effectively targeted through direct mail.

For many types of publication, bookshops are the last places likely customers are going to look for what they want.

A word of warning: it is always hard (for experienced

publishers as well as the inexperienced) to gauge how long a print run should be (i.e. how many copies to print). A long print run can begin to look like very good value, but if the book doesn't sell you can end up with an awful lot of copies to store and then dispose of. A short run, on the other hand, can put up the unit cost of each book considerably, and might price it out of the market it is aimed at.

Buying Remaindered Books

You may get your first chance to see how the business works if your existing publisher decides to remainder a book you have written for them.

Remaindering means selling off the remaining copies at next to no cost because the publishers don't believe they are going to sell any more through the normal channels. The author always gets first refusal on remaindered copies, and can then try selling them in any way possible. It is surprising how successful many authors have been with titles aimed at specialised targets which the publishers simply don't know about, or don't have the manpower to pursue.

Buying remaindered stock costs very little, and provides authors with a cheap way to test their marketing skills.

Doing Deals with Publishers and Distributors

You don't, of course, have to organise every part of the operation completely on your own. You could undertake to produce the books, and then offer a publisher a percentage of the takings to distribute them under their imprint. The publishers are happy because they get the book free (no printing, editing or writing costs), and you are happy because you get the bulk of the money.

Alternatively, you could cut the publisher out altogether, put your own imprint on the book and get a distributor to handle it.

In either case you would end up with about half the retail price of the book coming back to you, as opposed to the ten per cent or so which you would get as a royalty. How much profit you make will depend on how much you pay to get the books produced, and the number you manage to sell through your publicity and promotional skills.

What you don't get by publishing yourself, of course, is the advance. You actually have to invest money at the beginning of the project in the hope of reaping a return later on, the role normally taken by publishers rather than writers.

If the book is a success, however, you stand to make more than if you take the traditional route, because there are fewer people getting a share of the money. You may also find that the money comes in quicker, since the accounting systems of the established publishing companies are notoriously slow to pay writers.

MAGAZINES

If you are able to publish magazines as well as write them, you are broadening your potential market beyond recognition. This may come about because you happen to have the necessary design and production skills, or you may need to find other people who can provide these services.

Many highly successful magazines have grown out of the enthusiasm of writers who have decided to start up titles in their back bedrooms. Some of these publications are produced and sold with such energy that they grow to be full-sized titles and end up being bought out by major publishers. You might start with a pop fan magazine, or a hobby magazine for golfers or train spotters. It doesn't matter what the subject matter is as long as it is something you feel passionately about, and which fills a gap in the market.

Company Magazines

If you can get a contract to publish a magazine for an organisation like a company, association or union, you are likely to make a great deal more money than if you were simply commissioned to write for it.

You could also make the difference between the magazine existing or not. There are many organisations which like the idea of producing their own magazine or newspapers, but lack the manpower to do it. If you can offer them a complete package, they are more likely to decide to go ahead.

Some in-house magazines can grow into major publishing ventures. The airline publications, for instance, which are slotted into the backs of passengers' seats, have grown up to be as thick and glossy and full of advertising as any consumer titles on the newsagents' stands. Likewise, publications which are given away to customers in shops, banks or building societies, guests in hotels, or even to passengers on railways, all have their roots in the humble house magazine of days gone by.

However the sophistication of these titles doesn't mean that there isn't still a market for a more modest product to suit a more modest backer. Whether a publication is aimed at employees or customers or other opinion-forming groups, it needs to convey relevant information to the target readership and be written and produced to the highest possible standards.

Creating a magazine involves a number of tasks:

- Liaising with the client/sponsor to get the job in the first place, and then keep it.
- Doing the costings to ensure that you make an adequate profit and give the client a competitively priced service.
- Finding the stories, writing them and getting them approved by the sponsor.
- Organising photography, or doing it yourself.
- Finding a designer, or doing the design work yourself.
- Finding a typesetter and printer, keeping control of costs and overseeing the production process.
- Editing and laying out the publication.
- Commissioning other writers if necessary.
- Dealing with the physical distribution of the magazine.
- Selling advertising space, if appropriate.

The more of these jobs you do yourself, the more of the money will come to you. However there are bound to be some areas where you are less able or less experienced. By trying to keep it all to yourself you could end up limiting the quality and scope of your operation.

Building a Magazine Business

You could start out by selling your skills as a freelance writer but soon find that it is more profitable, and possibly more fun, to concentrate on the marketing side of the business, hiring other writers to produce the magazines for your clients.

If you manage to persuade half a dozen sizeable companies to give you contracts to produce their house magazines, you won't have time to write all the material yourself. You might still have your name in the magazine as editor but you are going to have to hire other people to do the legwork.

This is the first step towards building a company. For some writers the whole idea is anathema, since all they want to do is write, and the last thing they want is to become businesspeople. In that case it's perfectly possible to keep the company small, so that you can do all the writing and other work yourself. Alternatively, you could continue doing as much writing as you want, and hire other people to do the marketing or whatever else is required. There is also no reason why you shouldn't keep on writing for the magazines which interest you the most, and delegate the more mundane subjects to your employees.

NEWSLETTERS

As I have already mentioned, information and ideas are the stock-in-trade of the freelance writer. If you manage to compile a great deal of useful information on any one subject, a newsletter can be a highly profitable way of marketing it.

Newsletters, in their ideal form, are magazines where the editorial is of such high value to the readers that they are willing to pay large sums of money to gain access to it. Because the information is of such high value, the publisher's incomes do not need to be padded out with advertising revenues. They can make a profit simply by selling subscriptions.

The major selling point for most newsletters is the speed with which they are produced. They might for instance, be for the building industry, listing contracts which are coming up for tender. Any building company which doesn't want to be left behind by the competition will need this information as early as possible so that they can prepare their bids and make their marketing pitches to the client companies. If a building contract is worth several million, they are not going to worry about paying a few hundred, or even a few thousand, for a newsletter which brings them the necessary information quickly. The same principles will apply in any time-sensitive business, like the oil industry, for instance, or any of the financial services.

Newsletters can also be very successful in other sectors and if you have regular access to any information which would be of use to other people, then you have a potential market for a newsletter. It won't matter how crudely printed it is – as long as they can read it – and customers may even believe that the information is somehow 'hotter off the press' if the format looks rushed.

As well as the information itself, you also need lists of prospective customers for direct mail. You could send them one copy of the newsletter to show them what they will get for their money, or a well-worded mailshot explaining what opportunities they will miss if they don't subscribe.

You will have to price your newsletter according to what your average customers are likely to be able to afford, balanced against the potential worth of the information to them.

Once you have the two vital ingredients of content and customers, you can build the letter as slowly or as fast as you choose. If you get the formula right, it won't be long before you have a thriving business, and you will find yourself receiving offers from major publishing companies.

With developments in desk-top publishing technology, it has become possible for freelance writers to design, edit and produce their own newsletters (and indeed magazines and books). Discussing the pros and cons of the various desk-top publishing systems is outside the remit of this book. However anyone who has a publishing project in the pipeline, or actually under way, should explore all the available options, one of which is investing in a computer which will enable them to execute much of the production work themselves.

20

Money

So now we get to the heart of what this book is all about. How do you make sure that all this activity results in reasonable income? If you can't get this part of the business right, you won't be able to continue being a writer for long, unless you have an unearned income or a spouse who is willing to support your hobby.

WORKING OUT YOUR COSTS

The first step is to work out the cost of setting yourself up in the business as a writer.

Capital Expenditure

I touched on the sort of equipment you will need in Chapter 2, but it's worth recapping here, so that you can assess how much money you are going to need, and where you might be able to cut corners.

Firstly, you need a room where you can work undisturbed, which has a telephone line. It could be a spare bedroom or a shed at the bottom of the garden, a stately book-lined study or a shared office in your nearest town. It's better if it requires no outgoings beyond the normal household heating and lighting bills.

Next, you need a basic word-processor (you need spend no more than £1,500 to get the latest model), or a typewriter if that is all you can afford, an answering machine/fax, a tape-recorder (if you plan to do any interviewing) and stationery. The stationery has to include headed notepaper and business cards, envelopes of various sizes and reams of plain typing paper (photocopier paper is quite good enough). Never buy rough notepads; you will have plenty of spare paper if you use the backs of discarded manuscripts and letters.

None of this needs to be enormously expensive. Assuming there is a suitable room in your house, and that you already have a telephone installed, a total outlay of £500, excluding the word processor and answering machine/fax, would more than adequately launch you. If you don't have £500 then that will sound like a lot of money, but if you have any business experience at all you will appreciate just how little it is.

Many of these things you may be able to pick up secondhand, borrow from other people or persuade someone to give to you as Christmas or birthday presents. That could cut the costs by as much as half. If necessary you may have to borrow some of the money from your bank manager, but you must try to borrow as little as possible at the beginning. It will be some months before any money comes back in, and the interest rates could cripple you before you start.

Regular Outgoings

Stationery and services like faxing, printing, photocopying and postage will be the major expenses at the beginning, when you will be continually writing to people and sending them samples of your published work.

You might decide to have a leaflet or brochure printed, or to take advertising space somewhere – how much you spend on these items will depend on how much you have in the bank. Do not borrow money for these sorts of activities. If you can't pay for them out of your cashflow then you aren't ready to indulge in them; stick to direct mail.

Telephone bills will be the next item to consider. You are going to have to talk to people one way or the other. The telephone is expensive but it is a great deal cheaper than the petrol or train fares needed to meet people in person. At the beginning, when you are trying to keep costs down, do all the interviewing you can over the phone.

You will, however, have to meet some people and research some things in person, so you will need to allow for travel costs. If you already have a car then you will know roughly how much a certain mileage per year is going to cost you. If you don't have a car you will have to take some educated guesses as to what your train, bus and cab fares are likely to mount up to. Keep unnecessary trips to the minimum, and wherever possible get someone else to pay your expenses.

If you have been commissioned by a magazine ask them, at the time of commissioning, what expenses they will pay. Their reactions will vary from naming an amount to agreeing to pay travel expenses, to refusing to pay anything at all. If the job involves travel then it is quite in order to expect them to reimburse fares and accommodation costs. If it's a home-based job they may still pay for telephone calls.

If the assignment involves international travel, with air tickets and hotels, it is reasonable to expect them to make all the arrangements and send you the documents, although they will be delighted if you volunteer to do all the administration yourself. If you are commissioned to do an article which will involve a lot of outgoings it would be reasonable to ask for the expenses in advance. Unless it is a blue-chip publication, make sure you have some sort of agreement in writing before you pay out too much from your own pocket (unless you are confident of selling the article profitably to someone else, should the original commissioner go out of business or try to get out of the agreement).

For business writing you should usually be able to include expenses on your invoice, but check first, just in case.

For major travel projects there are a number of people who may help defray costs (see Chapter 15).

A book publisher might agree to pay expenses on a project they are really keen on, but it is not standard practice, and anything you sell speculatively to anyone will have to be researched at your own expense.

WORKING OUT HOW MUCH YOU NEED TO EARN

Ask yourself how much you want to give up in order to launch yourself into this new career. Do you, for instance, have a mortgage and school fees to pay? If so, can you afford to keep up the payments from your savings if you don't make any money for a year? If you can't, then you would be wise to change your circumstances to fit your likely new income – move house or change the kids' schools if necessary.

If you have some definite commissions lined up from the beginning, then you will know what your income is likely to be for the first six months and you can budget accordingly. If you are setting out from scratch you cannot expect to earn anything for at least six months, and you need to know how you will survive for a year on virtually nothing. The chances are that it will not be that bad, but you need to know how you would cope if it *was* that bad. It is no good thinking you will give writing a try for a few months, because you will never get it going in that time. It requires a long-term commitment.

So, make a list of all your usual household expenses – things like mortgage, heat and light, water, telephone, food, clothes, insurance – and add on something for extras like holidays and presents.

Then work out exactly how much income you need to maintain your lifestyle at the minimum level acceptable to you and any dependants you may have.

Having worked out your living expenses you may realise that you have to maintain at least some income from another source during the early months. You might be able to do this by easing your way slowly out of your existing job, or by taking a series of part-time jobs. Whether you're waiting on tables, serving behind bars, or doing messenger work, as long as you still have enough time and energy to write, it doesn't matter what else you do, although the more interesting you find it the better.

HOW MUCH CAN YOU HOPE TO EARN?

Now ask yourself honestly how much you can realistically hope to earn from writing in the first year or two. There's no point in being too ambitious to start with, because you are going to use this figure to set your rates, and if your rates are too high you won't get any work at all.

So let's say, just as an example, that you have decided the minimum you can live on is £10,000 a year. You might, therefore hope to earn £20,000 in the second year. Guessing that you will have to work at least fifty weeks a year, five days a week, that will mean earning £80 a day.

You won't, of course, be earning every day of the week to start with – or you may be doing work which will earn money later but which can only be treated as speculative at the beginning. So you need to earn more than this daily rate whenever possible in order to compensate for the days when you are writing selling letters, or doing research or speculative work.

Without being unrealistic, you should add as much of a margin to the daily rate as you think the market will bear, but it is always better to start low and ensure that you get the work in the beginning. There will be plenty of time for risk-taking later on.

HOW WILL YOU GET PAID?

Payment per Thousand Words

Newspaper and magazine editors will ask how much you want per thousand words. In most cases they will tell you what they pay, and you will just have to accept it, but you still need to know what price it is viable to work at.

Let's say that you can hope to write 2,000 words a day, but you need another day to research an article of that length. That will mean that you need to be paid at least £160, or £80 per thousand words. That is by no means unrealistic at the time of writing and in many cases you would be paid two or even three times that much. As you become more experienced you will be able to cut down the research time on many of your jobs, until you can do some of them with a couple of telephone calls and complete them in one day rather than two, thereby doubling your earning potential.

What do you do, however, if you are commissioned to write a book of 50,000 words and they offer you an advance of £2,000? Obviously you hope it will earn a great deal more than that for you in the long run, but supposing it doesn't? At £80 per thousand words you would need a minimum of £4,000 to reach your average daily wage on such a project, with no time for research. You want to take the job, but how do you make it financially worthwhile?

There are several alternatives. One is to write very fast indeed (say 4,000 words a day), though the quality of your work might suffer, not to mention your health. The second is to choose a subject which you already have the necessary background material for, to avoid spending time on research. The third is to supplement the writing of the book with other, better-paid work such as business and public relations writing or journalism. The fourth is to look for other ways of selling the research you are doing on the book, such as articles or public relations opportunities.

What you can't afford to do at the beginning is turn work down, however badly paid it might seem. You need to establish a track record first, then you can start to put your fees up.

The Going Rates

The going rates vary enormously and, although there are some standard rates set by professional associations and unions, the fact is that everyone gets what they can. To charge £100 a day for a reasonably short working day would not be unreasonable for a relative beginner, whereas somebody with an established reputation might ask for three times that amount. A star from television or the national press can virtually name their own price. If you can work out where you are on the scale, then those are the rates you should ask for, while still being prepared to drop to your basic figure rather than lose the work.

On the whole, business clients will be most comfortable with a daily rate, while editors will expect to pay a set rate per thousand words. In both cases it is sometimes possible to negotiate an overall fee for the whole job. The best way to do this is to estimate the amount of time you think the work will take, apply your standard daily rate to that, and then add on as large a margin as you think you can get away with, to allow for delays, rewrites and general mishaps.

Book publishers, film and television producers and other buyers will generally know what they are willing to pay, or, if you have a hot property on your hands, will be willing to haggle. This is where an agent might be useful (see Chapter 17), unless you are particularly skilled at negotiating, and have a clear idea of the market value of what you are selling.

Advances and Royalties

Once a book publisher has decided to publish your book, they will offer you royalty terms. A royalty is a payment made to the author per copy sold. It is calculated either as a percentage of the retail price of the book or as a percentage of the sum the publisher receives (after discounts given to distributors, booksellers and others). The most common royalty payments at present are ten per cent for a hardback and seven and a half per cent for a paperback.

The publisher may also offer you an advance against royalties which you will be allowed to keep, regardless of how many copies of the book they sell. Once the royalties owed to you exceed the amount you have been paid in advance, you will receive a payment once every six months based on the number of copies which have been sold.

Non-fiction tends to pay more than fiction, but few books will make you much money at the beginning of their lives. The chances are that a first-time writer will be offered an advance which is little more than an average month's income. It might be as little as a week's income, or as much as three months, but it is unlikely to be more than that.

To make matters worse, the publishers won't offer to pay the whole amount immediately. You will probably get a third on signing the contract, a third on delivering the manuscript and the final third on publication. The first and the last payments could be as much as a year apart.

If your first book is a success you will be in a stronger position to bargain for more money upfront on the next one – but you still won't be able to get very much more. So why, you might ask, are you always reading newspaper articles about those enormous, multi-million-pound advances for books?

Well, the very fact that they get reported in the papers shows that these sorts of payment are not exactly commonplace. They are more often associated with mass market fiction. And they are usually only given to non-fiction writers who are already famous or who have truly remarkable stories to tell on subjects which have guaranteed mass market appeal, such as books about the royal family or the most fashionable showbusiness and sports stars, or a newsworthy scandal or exposé.

Every now and then a professional writer will get hold of a story which commands more money than usual, and each opportunity has to be exploited to the full, but the average book does not give you this sort of bargaining power.

The very large advances which some publishers have been paying to a handful of writers are viewed as dangerous by many in the business. The publishers are either gambling that a book will be a best-seller and will earn back the money, or they are bribing a well-known writer to join their stable in order to add prestige to their list.

In either case it makes bad business sense for any company to pay out money before they have earned it. But it is very good business for the writers, since a big advance acts as publicity for the book concerned and ensures that the publishers will work hard to earn their money back by selling as many copies as possible.

For most publishing projects, the advance will be little more than a token of faith on the part of the publisher, and an encouragement to the writer to keep going. When negotiating the advance, a publisher will point out that if the book is a success the writer will soon start getting royalty payments. The writer, on the other hand, will want to know how he or she is supposed to live while they are waiting for the publishing and selling process to happen.

With most publishing projects, this is exactly what you are doing, building yourself a back-list of books which will go on earning you small amounts year after year after year. The books you wrote five years ago should eventually start supplementing the advances for books you are writing this year and so on. If you keep producing a flow of steady-selling books it should gradually create a snowball effect.

Bonuses

By working out the minimum daily rate you need to earn, you are not allowing for occasional bonuses which will compensate for the times when projects fail to sell or are rejected at some stage of their development.

For instance, you might be able to re-sell an article you wrote a few months ago (with only an hour or two spent on adapting), thereby adding £200 to that day's earnings. Or if you have written a number of books you might suddenly find that translation rights to one of them have been unexpectedly sold to a country in Scandinavia, and a few thousand pounds arrives out of the blue.

These sorts of occurrences gradually become more common as you get more experienced and increase the library of work you have to sell. Unfortunately, it is at the beginning, when money is tightest, that they happen least often.

KEEPING TRACK OF YOUR EARNINGS

As you progress you need to keep track of how well you are doing in order to make strategic decisions like whether to do more books and fewer articles, whether to concentrate on subjects which can be adapted for film or television, or whether to put most of your time into supplying reliable sources of revenue like trade magazines. You also need to decide whether you can afford to advertise, or print brochures, or put time into a speculative project which is close to your heart, like a novel.

Keep a record of all money that comes in, and use that as the official total of your earnings. Don't kid yourself that you are earning what you have calculated would be possible if everything went as well as that one good week you had three months ago . . . Be honest with yourself, and only count money which has actually gone into your bank account as truly safe.

By the end of the first year you should be able to see clearly the sort of income you can expect to make in the next six months. You will be able to see if there has been a month-upon-month increase. It will never be a steady upward curve, but it should show you the rough trend.

Measure Your Results Each Month

At the end of the year add up the total amount you have received in the last year. Then, at the end of each following month, work out how much you have earned in the previous twelve months. Keeping a running chart of these monthly 'annual results' will give you a clear idea of what your real average income has been and is likely to become.

If you look at the periods of less than a year you will find the figures too erratic. Some months you will earn nothing; other months you might earn enough to keep you going for three or more months. Only by looking at the longer-term trends can you assess your true situation.

By the end of the second year you should be earning at least the amount you hoped to earn at the beginning, and your graph should be showing upward movement, even if it is somewhat jerky. If you haven't reached that sort of speed by then, you should do some serious soul-searching as to whether you are in the right business, or whether you have got some part of your basic strategy wrong.

DRAWING UP A BUSINESS PLAN

If you want to borrow money from a bank they will want to see some sort of business plan. Your accountant, if you have one, can advise you on how to present the information to the bank manager. However you may also find it very useful to draw up a business plan for yourself. Essentially the plan needs to explain, in realistic terms, how you are going to survive as a freelance writer. It needs to answer the following questions:

- Who will give you work?
- How will you persuade them to give it to you?
- How much do you need to earn in order to live?

- How much are you likely to be paid by your prospective customers?
- How much do you need to spend to set yourself up (buying a word-processor, stationery etc, and any marketing expenses like postage or travel?
- How long will it be before the money starts to come in?
- Do you have any other income you can rely on while waiting for the money to arrive?
- How will you use the incoming money to get more work and increase your earning power?
- What are your goals, both in the short term (say, in a year) and in the long term (say, in ten years)?

KEEPING THE CASH FLOWING

All too often businesses go under because they don't have that magic ingredient, cashflow. Although their long-term prospects are fine, with lots of happy customers and the promise of more work in the future, the money does not come in fast enough, the debts pile up and eventually someone, in the form of a creditor or a bank manager, calls a halt.

To avoid this situation, you need to ensure that more money is coming in than going out, almost from day one. It sounds obvious, but it is surprising how many people have no idea how much money they have in the bank at any one moment, or how much they are owed.

Before you can decide what you can spend this month, you need to know how much money you can reasonably expect to come in over the next two months. That does not mean you can make up wonderful sums that may or may not come in from royalties, nor can you include the promise of a film sale from a producer you met in the pub last week. This is money for work which has been completed satisfactorily and which you have already invoiced for.

You need to keep a running total of how much you have in the bank, what has been invoiced for, and when it is likely to come in. By looking at your average monthly outgoings for the previous twelve months, you should be able to see whether or not you are going to be left with a surplus at the end of next . month and the month after that. If so, you can decide how to spend it – do you want to buy some advertising, take the family on holiday, or take a couple of weeks to do some speculative work which only has an outside chance of selling?

As you become more experienced, and as you take on more long-term projects like books, you will be able to extend that two-month period to as much as six months. It is unlikely that you will ever be able to see further into the future than that. But by the time you are that established you will have a good idea of what you can expect to earn each year.

Chase Invoices

Always include an invoice for the agreed amount when you send in the completed work. (For more about invoicing, see p.212.) Address the invoice to the editor who commissioned you or agreed the purchase.

A couple of weeks later, ring the accounts department of the company concerned to check that the invoice has got through to them. If it has, ask them when it is likely to be paid, and then make a note to ring again if it hasn't arrived a few days after the date they give. Get the name of the person you have spoken to, so that you can ask for them personally next time.

If the invoice hasn't got through to the accounts department, and if you know that your contact was happy with your work, ring them and ask them what has happened to the invoice.

Ask if they need a statement. Some companies have a policy of only paying bills when the statements arrive. You need to know that, otherwise you may be waiting in vain for them to pay upon invoice.

Many companies have set procedures, such as not paying until six weeks after publication. It is annoying at the beginning to have to wait so long for your money, but provided you keep a close watch on the figures and survive the first few months, you will soon adjust to it.

Mix Long-Term and Short-Term Projects

Try to have a mix of projects on the go. For instance, you might be doing some public relations work and articles which will only take a few days to complete, and will be paid for within a month or two. Mixed in with these, you could have books and scripts which might not bring in any income for a year or more, but may then go on earning for years or even decades.

By keeping this sort of balance you can satisfy your immediate income requirements, while expanding the business year upon year.

Bad Debts

If you are doubtful about the credentials or financial stability of someone who is commissioning work from you, be very careful about what you commit yourself to. Don't agree to undertake a project which will involve you in a great deal of personal expense, unless they will advance you some money to cover costs.

If they do go bust, the first you will hear about it will usually be a letter from the receivers telling you that you might get one pence in the pound if you are extremely lucky. Forget about it, because you will never get a penny, and will only waste time and nervous energy fretting about it. Instead immediately start trying to recoup your losses by selling the material to other people. If they have already published your article you will not be able to sell it to any directly competing journal.

HOW MUCH WILL YOU EARN?

How much you eventually earn will, as in any field of endeavour, depend partly on your skill at creating the product itself, and partly on your ability to manage your time and market your products successfully. If you are good at one of these elements, and average at the other you will survive. If you are bad at both of them then you need to think of something else to do. If you are good at both of them the sky is the limit.

21

Tax and the Law

These are the sorts of subjects which we all prefer not to think about when we first go freelance. To anyone who is inexperienced in either, they seem like minefields of complex rules and regulations, not to mention expense. Although I have no statistics to prove it, I suspect that the prospect of having to deal with the legal and taxation professions actually puts many people off becoming self-employed at all.

In reality, you will soon grow used to dealing with the more common aspects of both disciplines, and the more complex aspects can generally be avoided, or never crop up at all.

WRITERS AND THE LAW

Contracts

Working on the principle that the less you have to do with representatives of the legal profession the better off you are likely to be, it is always worth keeping contracts as simple as possible, or avoiding them altogether.

When you undertake to do a job for a magazine or newspaper editor you will normally be able to get by on a verbal agreement over the telephone as to what is expected of you, and what you expect to be paid. If you feel there is any possibility of a misunderstanding, then an exchange of letters just outlining what you have agreed should be enough.

Much the same applies to business writing projects. Letters of agreement are quite adequate, although you may need something more concrete if you are going to move on from just writing to publishing magazines, and will therefore be incurring costs on behalf of your clients.

If you are working for a publisher on a book project, for which you are being paid a one-off fee, then once again there is no need for anything more elaborate than a letter of agreement – unless they insist. If they do insist, then read the contract carefully and only consult a solicitor if you are suspicious about something.

At the beginning of your career, when you are trying to keep costs down and build relationships of trust with clients, you don't want to spend money on legal fees. If a client is trying to pull a fast one on you then you won't want to do business with them in the long term anyway.

I have sometimes done whole books for publishers without even a letter of agreement, and have never had any cause for complaint. The only danger with having nothing in writing is that the person you have dealt with might be taken ill or leave the company, and everyone else may claim total ignorance of whatever deal you have made with them.

While this situation is frustrating for you, the fact that they are acting in that manner suggests that you would be better off going to a company which plays straight and is keen on your project, rather than becoming entangled in a potentially long, bitter and expensive legal wrangle. If they are not keen to publish your book, then there isn't much point in forcing them to do so by law, since their hearts would not be in it and the project would be unlikely to thrive. Take it to someone else.

If you are going to be paid for a book with the standard system of royalties, with an advance against those royalties at the beginning, then you will need a contract, as the terms for these arrangements are very complex. Most publishers have standard forms, all of which are very similar, and you won't go far wrong by signing them on request and getting on with the job, particularly at the beginning of your career. If you are worried about the details, consult the books listed in the Bibliography under 'Contracts' and 'General Writers' Guides'.

As you become more established, and consequently more powerful, you might want to change certain clauses in the standard contract. You might, for instance, want to retain some of the subsidiary rights, or increase your royalty percentage. This is where you may need to bring in an agent or a solicitor to argue your case for you, to avoid a breakdown in your personal relationship with the publisher. By the time you get to this stage you will be able to afford such luxuries, and you will be in a stronger bargaining position because of your track record.

When it comes to selling film and television rights, you are entering territory which the legal profession has managed to make virtually impenetrable to the layperson. Here you will almost certainly need the advice of a professional, unless you are happy to sign whatever they put in front of you simply to get your hands on the advance, and you are willing to take the risk that you will be ripped off later if your project proves to be a box office hit.

Once again, there is a lot to be said for not expending time and money on the legal process at the beginning of your career, and concentrating your energies on the job of being a writer. It is, after all, more important for you to gain experience and a track record than money at this stage.

The problem with selling any subsidiary rights, including film and television, is that you are no longer dealing with individuals with whom you have a personal relationship. While you are negotiating with a magazine editor or a book publisher, you are forging bonds of mutual trust. Any betrayal of that trust will be personal, and is therefore less likely to happen. Legal departments of foreign publishers, buyers of serialisation rights, film producers and all the other potential customers for your projects are under no such obligation. In fact their jobs depend on getting as much as they possibly can out of contractual agreements and keeping as much money as possible for their employers or themselves. Get help when these situations arise.

When Should You Sue?

There may be occasions when you will consider suing one of the companies you are working for or with. Before you start proceedings you need to ask yourself the question: 'Am I likely to win enough money to compensate for everything that I am going to lose by being involved in a courtroom fight?'

All a writer has to sell in the end is his or her time, and the clarity of their thinking powers. If you become entangled in a long legal dispute you will have no time to conduct your other business. You will also be in danger of becoming bitter and obsessed with the one thing that has gone wrong in your life, at the expense of all the other things which were probably going fine.

If you truly believe that you are likely to win damages so substantial that all this sacrifice will be worth it, or if you feel there is a moral issue which simply can't be ducked, or if you have sufficient financial backing to be able to hand the whole business over to lawyers that you completely trust, then go ahead. But it is seldom worth it.

COPYRIGHT LAWS

You can't copyright ideas; you can only copyright the form in which they are presented. In other words, as soon as you commit your idea to paper, tape or film, in words or pictures, you are covered by copyright from having those words stolen.

It is, however, legitimate for you to quote someone else's work, provided you give them the necessary credit. But if you intend to quote at any length you need to check that you are not breaking the law. If you have someone else's book or article flattened out beside your word-processor, and you are lifting large chunks of their text and passing it off as your own work, then you are obviously cheating.

If you legitimately want to quote someone else's work at length, then write to them or their publishers, specifying which bits you want to use, why and where it will be published. Ask for their permission to quote the passage or passages concerned, and assure them that they will get full credit.

Some publishers, when approached, will ask for fees if you want to quote their authors' books. Unless you absolutely have to have that author's work in yours, I would suggest finding another source. Don't mention payment when you first ask for permission to quote another writer. Just stress how much publicity their work will get from being credited in your book (otherwise you may be putting ideas into their heads).

Plan ahead and if you think you might have to pay some permission fees, then make sure that this eventuality is covered in the contract with your publisher, so that they will pay at least part of the cost and preferably all of it.

LIBEL LAWS

In order to infringe the libel laws you have to write or say something about someone which is unmistakably about them and damages their reputation in some way. If you can prove that what you have written is true and fair comment, you will be in the clear. However if the person you have written about can prove that you have painted an inaccurate or misleading picture, then they will be able to get damages.

It may also be that someone you quote in a book or article libels someone in what they say. Again, you largely have to follow your own judgement. If he is the managing director of a supermarket chain and he is saying that a rival chain deliberately waters down their own-label drinks, or cheats the customers in some way, you can be sure that the accused supermarket is going to start suing everyone in sight, including you, your publisher and the interviewee.

If you have any doubts, ask your publisher if you can talk to their company's lawyers and get their advice. If this is not possible, and you are still worried, consult a solicitor yourself.

Your publisher's legal advisers will sometimes spot potential problems before an item is published, but they do expect you to take reasonable care to check your facts before handing the work in and, if you have a contract with them, they will have included a clause to that effect. If something slips past them, you will be liable and will then have to rely on their good nature to fight the case on your behalf. If the libelled party is serious about getting retribution they could well sue you and the publisher.

In most cases it is a question of common sense. Most of us know when we are attacking someone in a way which is likely to harm their reputation, and should then make sure that lawyers check the copy before it is published.

INCOME TAX AND ACCOUNTS SYSTEMS

The chances are that you won't have to worry about this for the first year at least, since you probably won't have enough income to pay any tax. However that does not mean you should let your accounts get into a mess. Accounts systems for writers don't have to be complex, but if they are not orderly you will end up wasting a lot of time trying to remember what money came from where and desperately hunting for receipts for anything that might be set against tax.

Keeping Accounts

When you complete each job, send the client an invoice which includes an invoice number, your VAT number (if you're registered for VAT), the date it's sent out, who it's for, what it's for and how much it's for. Keep a carbon or photocopy of every invoice you send out.

You also need to keep three lists:

1   A list of the invoices you send out in date order.

2   A list of payments that come in, month by month, with the date they arrive.

3   A list of all the expenses you incur in the course of your business (advertising, travel, stationery, postage, printing, telephone, etc).

Keep all the receipts for your expenses in date order, and put a reference number on each receipt to cross-refer to the list.

You should also keep your bank statements, cheque books (with the stubs filled in) and paying-in slips.

Whenever a payment comes in and you enter it in List 2, tick the relevant invoice off in List 1, to ensure that you don't forget it has arrived and send a statement by mistake.

Find out which your relevant tax authority is and let them know that you have gone freelance. Ask them what you should do about paying national insurance stamps, so that you can budget for the cost.

The tax authorities may be reluctant to accept that you should have self-employed status to begin with. If you are working extensively for only one employer they may claim that you are still fully employed and try to get PAYE tax out of you. Stand firm and show them all the things you are doing to get freelance work from a number of clients. Be as open as possible with them and explain exactly how you are intending to make your living. They will usually respond positively, and even helpfully, to anyone who is honest with them.

Choosing an Accountant

When the time comes to fill in tax forms, you will probably be able to do it yourself. However if you are uncomfortable about doing it, or simply don't want to spend the time, then find an accountant.

Go to see several accountants before you choose one, because you want to pick someone you like, who has experience of working with the self-employed, who will be able to grow with you over the years, and who will charge a reasonable rate. It can be highly inconvenient moving accountants at a later date, and a bad one can end up causing you just as much work as if you had done the job yourself.

A good accountant, however, will be able to prepare your accounts every year, and all you will have to do is send him or her your accounts records. They will charge an annual fee for this service, but they may also see opportunities for claiming back money which you would have missed, and which will justify their fees. Apart from anything else, it is just comforting to know that there is someone else on your side when those threatening-looking forms arrive through the post.

VAT

The threshold of turnover at which you have to register for VAT rises regularly, and it probably won't affect you for the first year or two. However you should find out what it is each year, and make sure you register as soon as your earnings in any one quarter exceed it.

If you don't register immediately, the VAT authorities will insist that you pay the VAT due from the time that you were first eligible, which you won't have claimed from your clients. That will mean you either have to find the money yourself – and if you are a year or more late in registering that could be a sizeable sum – or you will have to contact everyone you have invoiced during that period and ask them to send the extra money, which would be embarrassing and time-consuming.

Once you have registered, it is not difficult to keep a VAT system running. At one end you add 17.5 per cent (the current rate of VAT) to every invoice you send out, which clients can claim back (provided they are registered for VAT too, which almost all of them are).

At the other end, you keep a list of the VAT you have paid out on all the expenses you have been claiming against income tax. (Some things, like rail travel and books, are exempt so you need to find out the details from your VAT office.)

One mistake people often make is to calculate VAT on their expenses as 17.5 per cent of the total (as they do on their income). In fact the VAT has already been included on expenses so the total is, in effect, 117.5 per cent rather than 100 per cent. The simplest way to calculate the VAT on expenses (assuming you have a calculator) is to multiply the total by 7 and divide by 47.

Make it clear to the VAT office when you register that you would like to use the cash accounting scheme. This means that you pay up only on money received by you, not on money you have invoiced for. There are two systems and if you are on the wrong one you will be paying out the VAT before you have received it, and if you then suffer a bad debt it is hard to get the VAT refunded.

At the end of each three-month period the Customs and

Excise people will send you a simple form, which you fill in and return. It asks you to add up the amount of VAT paid to you during that period, and the amount which you have spent. You then deduct the smaller figure from the larger.

If you have earned more VAT than you have spent during that period you send the difference to Customs and Excise by the end of the following month. And if you have spent more than you have earned they will reimburse you the difference.

In 99 per cent of cases you will be sending them money. If you have earned nothing for three months, however, or if you have made some major capital expenditure on something like a new computer, then it could be the other way round, but if that is the case you need to look seriously at your cash flow. Unless you are owed one or two very large payments which simply haven't arrived yet, a situation like this could indicate that you have fallen below the VAT-able level again and you might need to find out about deregistering.

Provided you are doing your best to run an honest system, the VAT people will be very helpful if you have any enquiries. After you have first registered they may send an inspector out to check that you are keeping your accounts correctly. They are not trying to catch you out. In fact they might suggest ways in which you could be claiming more VAT rather than less.

Registering for VAT will actually save you money. The money you have to pay to Customs and Excise comes from your clients, on top of your normal income. Whereas you would previously have charged an editor £100 for an article, you merely add the VAT and charge them £117.50 with £17.50 going to Customs and Excise. The clients don't mind because they are claiming the extra back themselves (provided they are registered for VAT as well).

The VAT on your expenses, which you can claim back from Customs and Excise, you would previously have been paying out of your own pocket. For instance, say you buy a new computer and it costs £1,175 including VAT. If you are registered you will be able to claim back the £175; if not you have lost it. Being registered for VAT could easily save you between £1,000 and £2,000 a year just on normal business expenses, and much more if you are investing in equipment like computers.

Afterword

So, now you know as much as I do about making money from freelance writing. And within a few years you will probably have found out all sorts of things I haven't thought of − new ways to market work and new people to sell to.

If there is one golden rule I would impress on you, it is: 'NEVER, NEVER, NEVER GIVE UP.'

If you find you are constantly coming up against brick walls, look for other ways to approach things. Always be thinking laterally about new angles, new subjects to write about and new markets to sell to. And always have the needs of the customer clearly in your mind before you offer them any sort of proposition.

It may take longer than you hoped, to be able to support yourself by writing full-time, but once you are up and running you will find freelance writing the most varied, exciting and satisfying way to earn a living. On the other hand, if you just want to treat it as a useful sideline or hobby you will achieve many of the same satisfactions, and avoid some of the more nerve-racking elements.

Whichever you choose to do, I hope you will enjoy every minute of it.

Bibliography

Contracts

Clark, Charles, *Publishing Agreements* (Butterworths)

General Writer's Guides

Brande, Dorothea, *Becoming a Writer* (Papermac)
Directory of Publishing (Cassell and the Publishers Association)
Legat, Michael, *An Author's Guide to Publishing* and *Writing for Pleasure and Profit* (Hale)
Smith, Nancy, *501 Writer's Questions Answered* (Piatkus)
Turner, Barry, *The Writer's Handbook* (Macmillan)
Writers' and Artists' Yearbook (A & C Black)
Journalism
Baker, Donna, *How to Write Stories for Magazines* (Allison & Busby)
Clayton, Joan, *Interviewing for Journalists* (Piatkus)
Hennessy, Brendan, *Writing Feature Articles* (Butterworth-Heinemann)

Marketing and Publicity

Baverstock, Alison, *How to Market Books* (Kogan Page)

Self-Publishing

Finch, Peter, *How to Publish Yourself* (Allison & Busby)

Writing Books

Campbell, Morag, *Writing About Travel* (A & C Black)
Collier, Oscar with Frances Spatz Leighton, *How to Write and Sell Your First Novel* (Writers' Digest Books)
Geraghty, Margret, *The Novelist's Guide* (Piatkus)
Martin, Rhona, *Writing Historical Fiction* (A & C Black)
Smith, Nancy, *The Fiction Writers' Handbook* (Piatkus)
Smith, Nancy, *Writing Your Life Story* (Piatkus)
Taylor Pianka, Phyllis, *How to Write Romances* (Writers' Digest)

Writing for Film, Television and Radio

Schwarz, Lew, *The Craft of Writing TV Comedy* (Allison & Busby)

Useful Addresses

Magazines

The Bookseller, J. Whitaker & Sons, 12 Dyott Street, London WC1A 1DF, Tel: 0171 420 6000.
(Whitaker's also publish *British Books in Print.*)
PR Week, 174 Hammersmith Road, London W6 7JP Tel: 0171 413 4429
(*PR Week* is the trade magazine for the public relations industry.)
Publishing News, 43 Museum Street, London WC1A 1LY, Tel: 0171 404 0304.
Writers News, PO Box 4, Nairn, Scotland IV12 4HU, Tel: 01667 454441.

Directories

Advance Themetree Ltd, 2 Prebendal Court, Oxford Road, Aylesbury, Bucks HP19 3EY, Tel: 01296 28585.
(*Advance* lists details of forthcoming editorial features and supplements in the UK press.)

British Association of Communicators in Business Ltd (BACB), 2nd Floor, Bolsover House, 5/6 Clipstone Street, London W1PP 7EB, Tel/Fax: 0171 436 2545.
(BACB) produces a directory of all its members who are mainly editors of in-house magazines and newspapers.)

Hollis Press and Public Relations Annual, Harlequin House, 7 High Street, Teddington TW11 8EL, Tel: 0181 977 7711.
(*Hollis* carries comprehensive lists of public relations companies, in-house public relations personnel and other useful addresses.)

Kemps International Film, TV and Video Handbook, Variety Media Publications, 34-35 Newman Street, London W1P 3PD, Tel: 0171 637 3663. (The leading international production guide).

The Writer's Handbook, Macmillan Publishing, 25 Eccleston Place, London SW1W 9NF, Tel: 0171 881 8000.

Media Guides

The following companies all produce media guides listing editor's names, addresses and telephone numbers. Most of them produce regular up-dates to keep up with personnel moves. You need to ring round to find the one which will provide the most cost-effective answer to your requirements.

Benn's Media Directory, Miller Freeman Information Services, River Bank House, Angel Lane, Tonbridge, Kent TN9 1FE, Tel: 01732 362666.

Editor's Media Directories Ltd, 9-10 Great Sutton Street, London EC1V 0BX, Tel: 0171 251 9000.

PIMS UK Ltd, 12-15 Finsbury Place, London EC2M 7BT, Tel: 0171 588 1111.

PR Planner Ltd, Hale House, 290-296 Green Lanes, London N13 5TP, Tel: 0181 882 0155.

Index

Index